The Use of Preventive Detention Laws in Malaysia: A Case for Reform

M. Ehteshamul Bari • Safia Naz

The Use of Preventive Detention Laws in Malaysia: A Case for Reform

 Springer

M. Ehteshamul Bari
Thomas More Law School
Australian Catholic University
Melbourne, VIC, Australia

Safia Naz
Durham Law School
Durham University
Durham, United Kingdom

ISBN 978-981-15-5810-8   ISBN 978-981-15-5811-5   (eBook)
https://doi.org/10.1007/978-981-15-5811-5

This Springer imprint is published by the registered company Springer Nature Singapore Pte Ltd.
The registered company address is: 152 Beach Road, #21-01/04 Gateway East, Singapore 189721, Singapore

To our beloved parents, Mrs Umme Salma Atiya Bari and late Professor M. Ershadul Bari, for their undying love and limitless sacrifices.

Preface

Preventive detention is an extraordinary measure as it permits executive dispensation of the personal liberty of an individual on the mere apprehension that, if free and unfettered, he may commit acts prejudicial to national security or public order. Given the extraordinary nature of this power, it is, therefore, contended that the scope of the power should be confined to genuine emergencies threatening the life of the nation. Notwithstanding this, Article 149 of the Federal Constitution of Malaysia empowers the Parliament to enact preventive detention laws authorizing the executive branch of government to exercise the power of preventive detention without the precondition of an emergency. Furthermore, the Constitution does not stipulate adequate safeguards for mitigating the harshness of preventive detention laws. This book will make it manifestly evident that the weaknesses of the constitutional provisions concerning preventive detention have given the Parliament *carte blanche* power to enact a series of preventive detention statutes conferring wide powers on the executive to arbitrarily detain their political adversaries. Consequently, on the basis of this analysis, recommendations will be put forward for insertion in the Constitution detailed norms providing for legal limits on the wide power of the executive concerning preventive detention so as to ensure the maintenance of a delicate balance between protecting national interests and, simultaneously, observing respect for an individual's right to protection from arbitrary deprivation of liberty.

Melbourne, Australia   M. Ehteshamul Bari
Durham, United Kingdom   Safia Naz

Acknowledgements

This book could not have been written without the kind and generous support of mentors, colleagues and family members.

We would like to thank Professor David Weisbrot AM (Former President of the Australian Law Reforms Commission) and Associate Professor Johan Shamsuddin Bin Sabaruddin (Dean, Faculty of Law, University of Malaya) for their invaluable guidance and support.

We are profoundly grateful to our dearest mother, Mrs Umme Salma Atiya Bari, for her undying love and unconditional support. She has been the backbone of our family and words are not enough to express our gratitude to her. We also owe a profound debt of gratitude to our beloved father, late Professor M. Ershadul Bari (Former Vice-Chancellor, Bangladesh Open University, and Ex-Dean, Faculty of Law, University of Dhaka). He was our idol, and his teachings and lessons have guided all our academic endeavours.

Finally, Mrs Safia Naz would like to thank her husband, Sajal Rahman Azad, and son, Saafir Rahman Azad, for their love and support. M. Ehteshamul Bari would like to thank his wife, Samia Islam, for her constant support and encouragement.

Contents

1 **Introduction**... 1
   1.1 Introduction 1
   1.2 Safeguards Necessary for Constraining the Scope
      of the Power of Preventive Detention 3
   1.3 The Constitution of Malaysia and the Power of Preventive
      Detention 5
   1.4 Objectives of the Book.................................... 7
   1.5 Structure of the Book..................................... 8
   References... 9

2 **General Issues Concerning the Power of Preventive Detention
   and the Evaluation of this Power under the Federal Constitution
   of Malaysia, 1957**... 11
   2.1 Introduction 11
   2.2 Definition of Preventive Detention 12
   2.3 Necessity of the Power of Preventive Detention 13
   2.4 The Possible Abuse of the Power of Preventive Detention 15
   2.5 Evolution of the Power of Preventive Detention
      in Malaya during the British Rule 19
   2.6 The Constitution of Malaysia and the Provisions Concerning
      Preventive Detention 20
      2.6.1 Amendments to Article 149 of the Federal
         Constitution 23
      2.6.2 Critical Evaluation of Article 149 of the Federal
         Constitution 25
      2.6.3 The Constitutional Safeguards against the Abuse
         of the Power of Preventive Detention 27
   2.7 Changes Introduced to Article 150 of the Constitution 35
   References... 36

3   The Quest for a Standard Preventive Detention Framework   39
   3.1   Introduction   39
   3.2   The Right to Liberty and Permissibility of the Use
        of Preventive Detention under Human Rights Treaties
        and Various International Principles   40
       3.2.1   Safeguards as to Preventive Detention under
             the International Human Rights Norms   42
   3.3   The Guarantees Concerning Preventive Detention Contained
        in the 1973 Constitution of Pakistan and the 1996 Constitution
        of South Africa   47
       3.3.1   The 1973 Constitution of Pakistan and the Provisions
             Concerning Preventive Detention   48
       3.3.2   The Constitution of South Africa, 1996   51
   3.4   Developing a Standard Preventive Detention Framework   54
   References   58

4   Preventive Detention Laws in Malaysia & Their Use   61
   4.1   Introduction   61
   4.2   The Inadequacy of the Safeguards Concerning Preventive
        Detention Under the Federal Constitution of Malaysia   62
   4.3   Evaluation of the Provisions Concerning Preventive
        Detention in the ISA, SOSMA, PCA and POTA   64
       4.3.1   The Internal Security Act, 1960 (ISA)
             and the Purpose Behind Its Enactment   65
       4.3.2   The Security Offences (Special Measures) Act, 2012
             (SOSMA)   82
       4.3.3   The Prevention of Crime Act, 1959 (PCA)   89
       4.3.4   The Prevention of Terrorism Act, 2015 (POTA)   94
   4.4   Comparing and Contrasting the Preventive Detention
        Provisions of the SOSMA, PCA, and POTA with the ISA   106
       4.4.1   Use of Vague Terms and of Offences Criminalized
             Under the Ordinary Criminal Law as Grounds
             for Preventive Detention   106
       4.4.2   The Body Entrusted with the Power to Exercise
             Preventive Detention   106
       4.4.3   Maximum Period of Preventive Detention   107
       4.4.4   Access to Judicial Review   108
   References   109

5   Conclusion and Recommendations   113
   5.1   Introduction   113
   5.2   The Quest for a Standard Framework Concerning
        Preventive Detention   114
   5.3   The Adequacy of Malaysia's Constitutional
        Preventive Detention Framework   116

5.3.1   The Power of Preventive Detention Under
        the Malaysian Constitution   116
5.3.2   Key Characteristics of the Preventive Detention
        Laws in Malaysia...............................   117
5.4   Recommendations: A Constitutionally Entrenched
      Preventive Detention Framework for Malaysia Providing
      for Effective Safeguards..............................   120
References...   123

Table of Cases   125

Bibliography   127

Chapter 1
Introduction

Abstract The exercise of the power of preventive detention is considered an extraordinary measure. For it entails deprivation of an individual's liberty generally by an order of the executive for safeguarding national security or public order. Accordingly, light will first be shed, in this chapter, on the safeguards which have the merit of constraining the scope of the extraordinary power of preventive detention. Second, the enabling provision concerning preventive detention as contained in the Constitution of Malaysia will briefly be introduced. Third, the objectives of the book will be discussed. Fourth and finally, a summary of the chapters of this book will be provided.

1.1 Introduction

Preventive detention, also known as administrative detention, refers to the deprivation of an individual's liberty, either by order of the head of state or of any executive authority— civil or military— without that individual being formally charged or brought to trial before a court of law.[1] Such detention is preferred on the apprehension that if free and unconstrained, the individual concerned may commit acts prejudicial to the national security or public order. Thus, preventive detention is a precautionary measure aimed at preventing "mischief to the State".[2] However, it is also considered an extraordinary measure given it involves the executive dispensation of one of the most fundamental human rights, namely, the right to personal liberty, of an individual on the mere suspicion that, if not detained, he may commit an act endangering the security of the nation. In this context, the observations of Lord Macmillan in *Liversidge v. Anderson*[3] are noteworthy:

> The liberty which we so justly extol is itself the gift of the law and … may by the law be forfeited or abridged. At a time when it is the undoubted law of the land that a citizen may by conscription or requisition be compelled to give up his life and all that he possesses for

---

[1] International Commission of Jurists (1983), p. 394.

[2] *Rex v. Halliday* [1917] AC 260, p. 269.

[3] *Liversidge v. Anderson* [1942] AC 206.

© Springer Nature Singapore Pte Ltd. 2020
M. E. Bari, S. Naz, *The Use of Preventive Detention Laws in Malaysia: A Case for Reform*, https://doi.org/10.1007/978-981-15-5811-5_1

his country's cause it may well be no matter for surprise that there should be confided to the [executive]... a discretionary power of enforcing the relatively mild precaution of detention.[4]

In light of the objective underlying the exercise of the power of preventive detention, namely, preventing harm to the state, the international and regional human rights norms, such as those contained in the International Covenant on Civil and Political Rights, 1966 (ICCPR), the European Convention for the Protection of Human Rights and Fundamental Freedoms (ECHR), 1950, the American Convention on Human Rights, 1969 (ACHR), and the African Charter on Human and Peoples' Rights, 1981, acknowledge the right of state parties to use the power of preventive detention. However, these instruments do not provide state parties the blanket authority to exercise such power. Rather they seek to constrain the scope of the power by imposing an obligation on states to ensure that no one is detained arbitrarily.

Notwithstanding the utility of preventive detention, the extraordinary scope of the power often persuades the executive to misuse it during peacetime for political purposes. It is, therefore, necessary to stipulate adequate safeguards against the possibility of such abuse of the power. In Malaysia, the Constitution of Malaysia, which came into force in 1957, in Article 149 permits resort to preventive detention during peacetime for the maintenance of public order. Furthermore, the Constitution does not stipulate adequate safeguards for mitigating the harshness of preventive detention laws.

This book will make it manifestly evident that the weaknesses of the constitutional provisions concerning preventive detention have enabled succeeding generations of executives in Malaysia to use the wide powers concerning preventive detention under a series of preventive detention statues enacted by the Parliament for arbitrarily detaining their political adversaries. Consequently, on the basis of this analysis, recommendations will be put forward for insertion in the Constitution detailed norms providing for legal limits on the wide power of the executive concerning preventive detention so as to the ensure the maintenance of a delicate balance between protecting national interests and, simultaneously, observing respect for an individual's right to protection from arbitrary deprivation of liberty.

In this chapter, light will first be shed on the safeguards which have the merit of constraining the scope of the extraordinary power of preventive detention. Second, the enabling provision concerning preventive detention as contained in the Constitution of Malaysia will briefly be introduced. Third, the objectives of the book will be discussed. Fourth and finally, a summary of the chapters of this book will be provided.

---

[4] Ibid., p. 257.

1.2 Safeguards Necessary for Constraining the Scope of the Power of Preventive Detention

The exercise of the power of preventive detention, as discussed above, permits the curtailment of one of the most important human rights, namely, right to liberty, without any finding of guilt by a court of law. Accordingly, the International Commission of Jurists (ICJ) in its submission to the United Nations Human Rights Committee (HRC) prior to the drafting of a General Comment on Article 9 of the ICCPR observed that "'preventive detention' is, as a general matter, anathema to respect for human rights under the rule of law".[5] Consequently, taking into account the extraordinary nature of the power of preventive detention, the International Commission of Jurists (ICJ) in its submission to the Working Group on Arbitrary Detention had further opined that "a state may resort to preventive detention … to the extent strictly necessary to meet a threat to the life of a nation, and then only during a properly declared state of emergency".[6]

However, notwithstanding the adverse impact of the exercise of the power of preventive detention on the human rights of individuals, international human rights law does not stipulate that the scope of its exercise should be confined to genuine emergencies. Rather it merely stipulates that the exercise of the power of preventive detention must not be arbitrary.[7]

The absence of adequate safeguards against arbitrary detention under international human rights law has facilitated modern constitutional democracies to not circumscribe the exercise of the power of preventive detention to emergencies.[8] Subsequently, there has often been a tendency to use the power as a means for deterring "legitimate political dissent and to imprison people for the non-violent exercise of fundamental human rights such as the rights to freedom of expression and belief and to freedom of association".[9] Furthermore, human rights scholars contend that in the absence of safeguards for constraining the scope of preventive detention, the exercise of such power not only causes the violation of the right to liberty but also core rights, such as the right to life and the proscription on torture.[10] This argument is bolstered by reference to, for instance, the United States Senate Report on the various method of torture used by the Central Intelligence Agency (CIA) in Guantanamo Bay and the Report concerning the UK's Belmarsh Case. These reports

---

[5] United Nation Human Rights Committee (2013), https://www.ohchr.org/Documents/HRBodies/CCPR/GConArticle9/ICJ_GCArticle9.pdf

[6] United Nations Human Rights Council (2012), http://icj.wpengine.netdna-cdn.com/wp-content/uploads/2012/06/Submission-working-Group-detention-analysis-brief-2012.pdf

[7] Londras (2011), p. 36.

[8] Harding and Hatchard (1993), p. 6.

[9] Cook (1992), p. 11.

[10] Bari (2017a), p. 46.

demonstrate that indefinite or prolonged detention "often leads to inhuman treatment, death and certain forms of torture".[11]

Accordingly, it is necessary for national constitutions to guarantee certain safeguards for limiting the scope of abuse of the power of preventive detention. These safeguards can be summarized as follows:

(a) confining the use of preventive detention to declared periods of emergency;
(b) right of the detainee to be informed of the grounds of detention within the shortest possible timeframe;
(c) right of the detainee to make representation against an order of detention before a body independent of the wishes of the executive branch of government;
(d) right to protection from detention incommunicado, which means "nonpublication of the names of persons detained, denial of access to a court or to a lawyer, [and] denial of visits by family members"[12];
(e) right of the detainee to challenge the legality of order of detention in pursuance of a writ of *habeas corpus*;
(f) stipulation of a maximum time limit for keeping a detainee in preventive custody;
(g) right of the detainee to claim financial compensation in the event of an unlawful and arbitrary deprivation of liberty.

It will be argued in this Book that the incorporation of the above safeguards in a constitution ensures the maintenance of a delicate balance between the necessity to preserve national security and to simultaneously maintain respect for the right of individuals to be free from arbitrary detention. Justice Fazl Ali of the Indian Supreme Court shed light on the importance of maintaining such balance when he remarked in *AK Gopalan v. State of Madras*[13] that:

> I am aware that … in many countries, there has been reorientation of the old notions of individual freedom which is gradually yielding to social control in many matters. I also realize that those who run the State have very onerous responsibilities… Granting then that private rights must often be subordinated to the public good, is it not essential in a free community to strike a just balance in the matter? That a person should be deprived of his personal liberty without a trial is a serious matter, but the needs of society may demand it and the individual may often have to yield to those needs. Still the balance between the maintenance of individual rights and public good can be struck only if the person who is deprived of his liberty is allowed a fair chance to establish his innocence, and I do not see how the establishment of an appropriate machinery giving him such a chance can be an impediment to good and just government.[14]

The above safeguards also have the merit of guarding against the violation of core human rights of individuals, such the right to life and the right to freedom from torture, kept in preventive custody.

---

[11] Ibid., p. 52.

[12] Bari (2017b), p. 430.

[13] *AK Gopalan v. State of Madras* [1950] SCR 88 (India).

[14] Ibid., para 109.

1.3 The Constitution of Malaysia and the Power of Preventive Detention

The 11 territories of peninsular Malaysia joined together to form the Federation of Malaya in 1948 and eventually gained independence from the British on 31 August 1957. The first Prime Minister of the Federation of Malaya, and Malaysian *Bapa Kemerdekaan* (Father of Independence), Tunku Abdul Rahman, in his 'Proclamation of Independence' on 31 August 1957 at *Merdeka* Stadium in Kuala Lumpur declared that the new Federation 'shall be forever a sovereign democratic and independent State founded upon the principles of liberty and justice.'[15] On 16 September 1963, the decolonised Singapore, Sarawak and British North Borneo (now known as Sabah) joined the Federation of Malaya and the newly formed 14- State Federation was renamed Malaysia. Since Singapore left the Federation of Malaysia in 1965, Malaysia is now comprised of 13 states, and of three Federal Territories of Kuala Lumpur, Putrajaya and the island of Labuan.[16]

The Constitution of the Federation of Malaya, which was drafted by the Independent Constitutional Commission chaired by Lord Reid of the United Kingdom,[17] came into force on 31 August 1957- the *Merdeka* (Independence) Day. Subsequently, through the passage of the Malaysia Act, 1963, which amended Article 1(1) and 1(2) of the 1957 Constitution to, *inter alia*, admit three new states to the Federation and to rename the Federation as Malaysia, the Constitution was "introduced as the Constitution of Malaysia" on 16 September 1963— the Malaysia Day.[18]

However, it is pertinent to stress here that the objectives of preserving "a democratic way of life" and of upholding the supremacy of the Constitution and the rule of law which lie at the heart of the National Principles (*Rukun Negara*)— developed on 31 August 1970 to foster inter-racial harmony and unity— have not been incorporated into the Constitution of Malaysia by means of an amendment either as the Directive Principles of Policy, as can be found in the 1950 Indian Constitution, or as the Fundamental Principles of State Policy, as contained in the 1972 Constitution of Bangladesh.

Furthermore, unlike the Constitutions of other Commonwealth nations, the Malaysian Constitution does not even contain a preamble embodying the ideals and aspirations of the people, such as the establishment of a society based on democratic virtues, namely, the advancement of the rule of law and human rights.[19] In this context, the Preamble to the Constitution of Bangladesh deserves special attention. For

---

[15] Lee (1999), p. 5.

[16] US Department of State (2020), http://www.state.gov/r/pa/ei/bgn/2777.htm

[17] The other members of the Independent Constitutional Commission were Sir Ivor Jennings (United Kingdom), Sir William Mckell (Australia), B. Malik (India) and Justice Abdul Hamid (Pakistan). At the last moment, the Canadian nominee withdrew.

[18] Jewa et al. (2007), pp. 11–14.

[19] *In Re: Berubari Union Case*, AIR 1960 SC 845 (India).

it, among other things, stipulates that: 'it shall be a fundamental aim of the State to realise through the democratic process … a society in which the *rule of law, fundamental human rights and freedom, equality and justice*[20] … will be secured for all citizens.'[21]

However, the Independent Constitutional Commission did recommend the incorporation of certain fundamental rights, which are considered "essential conditions for a free and democratic way of life",[22] in the Constitution of Malaysia. Accordingly, the Constitution of Malaysia guarantees nine fundamental rights, labelled as "fundamental liberties", for the enjoyment of individuals. These include the right to personal liberty guaranteed under Article 5 of the Constitution. Notwithstanding such a guarantee, the Constitution itself contains provisions permitting the curtailment of the right to liberty during peacetime. Article 149 of the Constitution enables the Parliament to enact laws empowering the executive branch of the government to detain individuals for preventing the commission of activities subversive and prejudicial to the security of the nation. However, the Constitution does not stipulate adequate safeguards for mitigating the harshness of preventive detention laws. For instance, the Federal Constitution of Malaysia does not: (a) confine the exercise of the power of preventive detention to formally declared states of emergency but rather empowers the executive to exercise such power during peacetime; (b) prohibit detention incommunicado; and (c) specify a maximum time limit on keeping an individual in preventive custody.

This Book will argue that due to the weaknesses of the provisions concerning preventive detention contained in the Constitution of Malaysia, a series of preventive detention statues have been enacted by the Parliament. The Internal Security Act 1960 (ISA) was the first among these statutes, which remained in force for nearly 52 years until it was repealed in 2012, and it permitted the executive to keep individuals in preventive custody for indefinite periods.[23] Consequently, the wide powers concerning preventive detention under the ISA were used by succeeding generations of executives to indiscriminately keep the critics of their policies behind bars even during peacetime. Although the ISA was repealed in 2012 due to years of widespread abuse of the powers concerning preventive detention contained therein, several of its provisions have been brought back through the enactment of a series of security laws, namely, the Security Offences (Special Measures) Act, 2012 (SOSMA), the Prevention of Crime Act, 1959 (PCA), as amended in 2014 and 2015, and the Prevention of Terrorism Act, 2015 (POTA). It will also be shown that these laws, in some cases, are more draconian in nature than the ISA. Furthermore, light will be shed on the fact that the wide powers concerning preventive detention under some of these laws have already begun to be used by the executive in the same

---

[20] Constitution of Bangladesh, 1972 (Bangladesh), Preamble.

[21] Constitution of Bangladesh, 1972 (Bangladesh), Preamble, para 3.

[22] Federation of Malaya Constitutional Commission (1957), Chapter IX Fundamental Rights – Constitutional Guarantees, para 161.

[23] *See* Internal Security Act 1960, Art. 88 (Malaysia).

manner as it had been done under the ISA for victimizing its political adversaries. Thus, this book will make it evident that subsequent governments in Malaysia have relied on the extraordinary power of preventive detention to demonstrate their contempt towards democratic values, such as, respect for the rule of law and the basic rights of individuals.

1.4 Objectives of the Book

This book endeavours to fill a significant gap in the existing literature regarding the wide powers of the executive under various preventive detention laws, which have been enacted in pursuance of the *Federal Constitution of Malaysia* since the repeal of the ISA in 2012, and the exercise of these powers for purposes other than that of preventing threats posed to the security of the nation. In order to address the deficiencies of the constitutional provisions concerning the extraordinary powers of preventive detention, this book will, in part, rely on comparative constitutional analysis. In particular, this analysis will draw on the similarities in the exercise of preventive detention powers under the constitutional arrangements of similarly situated polities, and on the safeguards concerning preventive detention powers contained in the Constitutions of Pakistan and South Africa—which had been incorporated in order to avoid the experiences of past abuse of these powers in these jurisdictions. The comparative experiences of these jurisdictions will provide insight into the mechanisms necessary for ensuring a delicate balance between the necessity to prevent the state from being perished during threats posed to its security on the one hand, and to simultaneously uphold the fundamental human rights of individuals on the other.

The proposed book, therefore, will address the following question:

- What preventive detention framework in Malaysia would ensure the best possible means of maintaining an appropriate balance between protecting national interests during threats posed to the life of the nation and simultaneously upholding respect for an individual's right to protection from arbitrary preventive detention?

Since no systematic and structured research has so far been carried out examining the recently enacted preventive detention laws in Malaysia, namely the SOSMA, PCA, and POTA, and comparing their provisions with those of the repealed ISA, the proposed research will enhance knowledge by exposing the inadequacy of the safeguards stipulated by the Malaysian Constitution for mitigating the harshness of these laws. Consequently, based on these findings, recommendations will be put forward to rectify these defects from comparative constitutional law and normative perspectives. The outcome of this proposed book will not only establish the best means for obviating the possibility of the abuse of the powers concerning preventive detention but also for safeguarding humane treatment of individuals kept in preventive custody in Malaysia.

1.5   Structure of the Book

Following this chapter, the structure of this book will be divided into four chapters. In Chap. 2, titled 'General Issues Concerning the Power of Preventive Detention and the Evaluation of this Power under the Federal Constitution of Malaysia, 1957', light will first be shed on the general issues pertaining to preventive detention, i.e. the definition of preventive detention, the necessity for the exercise of the power and the possibility of its abuse. Second, this chapter will examine the evolution of the power of preventive detention in Malaya during the British rule. Third, it will discuss the evolution of the grounds stipulated in the Federal Constitution of Malaysia warranting the exercise of the power of preventive detention. Finally, it will critically examine the safeguards contained in the Constitution for mitigating the harshness of the exercise of the power of preventive detention.

Chapter 3, titled 'The Quest for a Standard Preventive Detention Framework', will in the first place seek to evaluate the safeguards afforded by various international and regional human rights instruments for preventing arbitrary encroachment on the liberty of individuals. Second, this chapter will shed light on the procedural safeguards contained in the Constitutions of some of the modern democracies, such as, Pakistan and South Africa, for constraining the scope of the exercise of the extraordinary power of preventive detention. Consequently, this chapter will embark on the endeavour to develop a standard preventive detention framework stipulating detailed norms for preventing the possibility of abuse of the powers concerning preventive detention and simultaneously guaranteeing the humane treatment of individuals kept in preventive custody.

Chapter 4, titled 'Preventive Detention Laws in Malaysia & Their Use', in light of the standard preventive detention framework developed in Chap. 3, will examine the weaknesses of the constitutional provisions in Malaysia concerning the exercise of the power of preventive detention. It will be demonstrated that the absence of adequate constitutional safeguards has paved the way for the enactment of a series of similar preventive detention laws, namely the ISA, SOSMA, PCA and POTA, which have in turn been used to substitute the ordinary criminal laws and to silence legitimate political dissent. The judicial response to such exercise of the power of preventive detention will also be discussed.

Finally, the concluding chapter, Chap. 5, in light of the standard constitutional model concerning preventive detention and the inadequacy of the preventive detention framework under the Federal Constitution of Malaysia, will put forward recommendations for insertion of adequate safeguards in the Constitution with a view to diminishing the possibility of abuse of the powers concerning preventive detention in Malaysia.

References

Bari, M. E. (2017a). Preventive detention laws in Bangladesh and their increased use during emergencies: A proposal for reform. *Oxford University Commonwealth Law Journal, 17*(1), 45–46.

Bari, M. E. (2017b). *States of emergency and the law: The experience of Bangladesh*. New York: Routledge.

Cook, H. (1992). Preventive detention – International standards and the protection of the individual. In S. Frankowski & D. Shelton (Eds.), *Preventive detention: A comparative and international law perspectives* (p. 11). Springer.

De Londras, F. (2011). *Detention in the 'war on terror': Can human rights fight back?* Cambridge: Cambridge University Press.

Final Report of Federation of Malaya Constitutional Commission (Reid Commission). (1957). Submitted on 21 February 1957.

Harding, A. J., & Hatchard, J. (1993). Introduction. In A. J. Harding & J. Hatchard (Eds.), *Preventive detention and security law: A comparative survey* (p. 6). Boston: Martinus Nijhoff Publishers.

International Commission of Jurists. (1983). *States of emergency: Their impact on human rights* 394.

Jewa, T. S., Buang, S., & Merican, Y. H. (Eds.). (2007). *Tun Mohammed Suffian's an introduction to the constitutional of Malaysia* (3rd ed., pp. 11–14). Pacifica Publications: Petaling Jaya.

Lee, H. P. (1999). Constitutional heads and judicial intervention. In W. M. Aun (Ed.), *Law in contemporary Malaysia* (p. 5). Petaling Jaya: Addison Wesley Longman.

United Nations Human Rights Committee. (2013). *International Commission of Jurists: Initial comments on draft General Comment 35 on Article 9 of the International Covenant on Civil and Political Rights*. Submitted 16 October 2013. http://www.ohchr.org/Documents/HRBodies/CCPR/GConArticle9/ICJ_GCArticle9.pdf

United Nations Human Rights Council. (2012). *International Commission of Jurists, submission to the working group on arbitrary detention: The definition and scope of arbitrary deprivation of liberty in customary International Law*. Submitted February 2012. http://icj.wpengine.netdna-cdn.com/wp-content/uploads/2012/06/Submission-working-Group-detention-analysis-brief-2012.pdf

US Department of State. (2020). *Background note: Malaysia*. Published 21 January 2020. http://www.state.gov/r/pa/ei/bgn/2777.htm

Chapter 2
General Issues Concerning the Power of Preventive Detention and the Evaluation of this Power under the Federal Constitution of Malaysia, 1957

Abstract The exercise of the power of preventive detention is considered an imperative necessity to adequately contain the dangers posed to the security and safety of nation. However, the extraordinary scope of the power often persuades the executive to use this power for extraneous purposes. Notwithstanding such a risk, Article 149 of the Federal Constitution of Malaysia empowers the Parliament to enact preventive laws, which authorize the executive to exercise the power of preventive detention without the precondition of an emergency. In this Chapter, an attempt will first be made to shed light on the general issues pertaining to the power of preventive detention. In particular, the definition of preventive detention, the necessity of the exercise of the power of preventive detention and the possibility of abuse of such power will be scrutinized. Second, the evolution of the power of preventive detention in Malaya during the British rule will be discussed. Third, an endeavour will be made to evaluate the provisions of the Malaysian Constitution permitting the enactment of preventive detention laws. Finally, the safeguards stipulated by the Constitution for mitigating harshness of preventive detention laws will be examined.

2.1 Introduction

The exercise of the power of preventive detention has become a common feature of the modern democracies. Since preventive detention entails dispensation of the liberty of an individual without any finding of guilt and without affording him an opportunity to have his day in a court of law, it is considered an extraordinary power. Given the extraordinary scope of the power, its use is usually justified for effectively dealing with the exigencies of a grave threat posed to the life of a nation, such as war or external aggression. As Lord Atkin in *Rex v. Halliday*[1] observed: "However precious the personal liberty of the subject may be there is something for which it may well be, to some extent, sacrificed by legal enactment, namely, national success in the war or escape from national plunder or enslavement."[2] Notwithstanding these arguments, the reality is that modern constitutions do not confine the exercise of the

---

[1] *Rex v. Halliday* (1917) AC 260.

[2] Ibid., pp. 271–272.

© Springer Nature Singapore Pte Ltd. 2020

M. E. Bari, S. Naz, *The Use of Preventive Detention Laws in Malaysia: A Case for Reform*, https://doi.org/10.1007/978-981-15-5811-5_2

power of preventive detention only to grave crises, as is evident from the provisions concerning preventive detention contained in the constitutions of many democratic nations. Rather these constitutions permit resort to preventive detention measures during peacetime. Consequently, there is a greater tendency among executives to use this power for detaining their political opponents.

An attempt will first be made in this chapter to shed light on the general issues pertaining to the power of preventive detention. In particular, the definition of preventive detention, the necessity of the exercise of the power of preventive detention and the possibility of abuse of such power will be scrutinized. Second, this chapter will discuss the evolution of the power of preventive detention in Malaya during the British rule. Third, an endeavour will be made to evaluate the provisions of the Malaysian Constitution permitting the enactment of preventive detention laws. Finally, the safeguards stipulated by the Constitution for mitigating harshness of preventive detention laws will be examined.

2.2   Definition of Preventive Detention

The term "preventive detention" has its origin in the language used by the judges or the Law Lords in England while explaining the nature of detention under Regulation 14 (B) of the Defence of Realm Consolidated Act 1914, which was passed following the outbreak of the First World War. Lord Finlay expounded the meaning of preventive detention in the landmark case of *Rex v Halliday*[3] by terming it as a measure taken "against dangers … impos[ing] some restriction on the freedom of movement of persons whom there may be any reason to suspect of being disposed to help the enemy."[4] It is evident from this observation that preventive detention does not take the form of punishment. Rather it is aimed at intercepting an individual before he gets the opportunity to commit a prejudicial act. As Lord Atkin observed in *Rex v. Halliday*[5]:

> Preventive justice … consists in restraining a man from committing a crime he may commit but has not yet committed, or doing some act injurious to members of the community which he may do but has not yet done … [P]reventive justice proceeds upon the principle that a person should be restrained from doing something which, if free and unfettered, it is reasonably probable he would do, it must necessarily proceed in all cases, to some extent, on suspicion or anticipation as distinct from proofs.[6]

Thus, "the measure [of preventive detention] is not punitive but precautionary".[7] However, preventive detention is not merely a precautionary measure. Rather, as pointed out above in Sect. 2.1, it is also an extraordinary measure given the significant burden imposed by the executive on the liberty of an individual because of the

---

[3] *Rex v. Halliday* (1917) AC 260.
[4] Ibid., p. 269.
[5] *Rex v. Halliday* (1917) AC 260.
[6] Ibid., pp. 273–275.
[7] Ibid.

suspicion that he may commit acts prejudicial to the security of the state or the maintenance of public order.[8] Justice Mukherjee in *A.K. Gopalan v. The State of Madras*[9] captured both aspects of the power of preventive detention, when he observed:

> the object of preventive detention is not to punish a man for having done something but to intercept him before he does it to prevent him from doing it. No offence is proved, nor any charge formulated and the justification is suspicion or reasonable probability and not criminal conviction which only can be warranted by legal evidence.[10]

In the 1980s, the International Commission of Jurists (ICJ) in a comprehensive Study on the States of Emergency, took notice of the wide scope of the power of preventive detention, when it defined preventive detention as "the deprivation of a person's liberty, whether by order of the Head of State or of any executive authority, civil or military, for the purposes of safeguarding national security or public order, or other similar purposes, without that person being charged or brought to trial".[11]

Therefore, in light of the above discussion, preventive detention can be defined as the denial of an individual's right to liberty by an order of the executive under enabling statutes for preventing the former from engaging in activities which are prejudicial to safeguarding national security or maintaining public order. It is not only a precautionary measure but also an extraordinary one which deprives the detainee of his fundamental right to liberty not as punishment for a transgression proven in a court of law but rather on the suspicion that he may pose a threat to the society.

2.3 Necessity of the Power of Preventive Detention

The necessity of resorting to the power of preventive detention is keenly felt during emergency situations, such as, war, external aggression, and armed insurgency, which truly endangers the security of a nation and necessitates swift actions for restoring normalcy.[12] For the ordinary criminal law, which requires evidence of actual commission of an offence for securing the conviction of an accused in a court of law, does not provide the executive with the necessary ammunition to detain an individual in an effort to prevent him from committing activities prejudicial to the safety and security of the state. By way of contrast, the power of preventive deten-

---

[8] Bari (2017a), p. 95.

[9] *A.K. Gopalan v. The State of Madras* [1950] AIR 27.

[10] Ibid., pp. 249–250

[11] International Commission of Jurists (1983), p. 394.

[12] The European Court of Human Rights in *Gerard Lawless v Republic of Ireland* [1961] E.Ct.H.R, Ser. A. No. 1 defined an emergency as "an exceptional situation of crisis or emergency which affects the whole population and constitutes a threat to the organised life of the community of which the State is composed".

tion by doing away with the procedural formalities associated with the ordinary criminal law, enables the state to take prompt action of a preemptive nature for averting the danger to its security.[13]

Although preventive detention amounts to deprivation of an important human right of a person—the right to liberty—it is considered essential for safeguarding the fundamental interests of other members of the society. In this context, the observations of Justice Patanjali in the case of *A.K. Gopalan v. The State of Madras*[14] are worthy of quote:

> This sinister-looking feature, so strangely out of place in a democratic Constitution, which invests personal liberty with the sacrosanctity of a fundamental right... is doubtless designed to prevent an abuse of freedom by anti-social and subversive elements which might imperil the national welfare of the infant republic.[15]

Thus, "the necessity of internment of a person solely by dint of executive order outside the framework of judicial process is dictated by the greater welfare of the society which is regarded as of supreme value—*salus populi suprema lex*". Accordingly, the regional and international human rights norms developed in the 1950s, 1960s and 1980s, such as the European Convention for the Protection of Human Rights and Fundamental Freedoms, 1950, International Covenant on Civil and Political Rights, 1966, and the American Convention on Human Rights, 1969, recognize the utility for state parties to exercise the power of preventive detention.

Historically, it has been a common practice for democratic nations to respond to emergencies through the enactment of specific statutes enabling the executive branch of government to exercise the power of preventive detention. However, these statutes would usually be repealed after the circumstances which led to their enactment ceased to exist. For instance, in the UK, wartime statues, such as the Defence of the Realm Act, 1914[16] and the Emergency Powers (Defence) Act, 1939, which empowered the executive to exercise the power of preventive detention, were repealed following the cessation of the first and second world wars respectively. Similarly, in the USA, the Emergency Detention Act, Title II of the Internal Security Act of 1950, which was enacted at the height of the Cold War for authorizing the federal government, among other things, to detain an individual suspected of espionage or sabotage, was ultimately repealed in September 1971 without being invoked on a single occasion. However, in stark contrast to these practices, some of the newly independent nations in Asia have not only permitted preventive detention statutes enacted in pursuance of relevant constitutional provisions to become a permanent feature of the legal system but have also enabled their use without the precondition of an emergency threatening the security of the nation. Consequently, the

---

[13] Bonner (1985), p. 2; Rudolph (1984), p. 12.

[14] *AK Gopalan v. State of Madras* [1950] AIR 27.

[15] Ibid, pp. 75–76.

[16] Although the Defence of the Realm Act, 1914 remained in force until 1921, the powers contained in the Act were never exercised to their "fullest coercive potential" Hynes (2017).

extraordinary power of preventive detention in these nations has often been used during peacetime for extraneous purposes.

2.4   The Possible Abuse of the Power of Preventive Detention

Notwithstanding the utility of the power granted to the executive branch of government under preventive detention statutes to unilaterally detain an individual during grave crises, the absence of meaningful safeguards regulating scope of the power often persuades the government of the day to misuse the power for furthering its parochial political agenda of consolidating grip on power by indiscriminately detaining political adversaries. In this context, the words of Lord Shaw of Dunfermline in *Rex v. Halliday*[17] are of particular significance. As he observed:

> Vested with this power of proscription and permitted to enter the sphere of opinion and belief, they, who alone can judge as to public safety and defence, may reckon a political creed their special care, and if that creed be socialism, pacifism, republicanism, the persons holding such creeds may be regulated out of the way, although never deed was done or word uttered by them that could be charged as a crime. The inmost citadel of our liberties could be thus attacked.[18]

The disturbing possibility of abuse of the power of preventive detention in the absence of meaningful safeguards has been manifested in the exercise of the power in various jurisdictions around the globe. In this context, reference can first be made to the exercise of the power of preventive detention under various statutes enacted under the Constitution of India, 1950. The Indian Constitution empowers the Parliament to pass laws concerning preventive detention "for reasons connected with Defence, Foreign Affairs, or the Security of India".[19] However, the Constitution does not detail the circumstances which can: (a) be prejudicial to defence; or (b) jeopardize India's relation with foreign powers; or (c) undermine the security of the state. Thus, the Supreme Court of India observed in *AK Roy v. Union of India*[20]: "Expressions like defence of India, "Security of India" … relations of India with foreign powers … are not of great certainty or definiteness."[21]

It is, therefore, striking that the Constitution of India does not expressly confine the exercise of the power of preventive detention to officially declared states of emergency. Furthermore, the Constitution does not stipulate the maximum period for which an individual can be kept in preventive custody. It seems that Indians after securing independence from the British rule had completely changed their views

---

[17] *Rex v. Halliday* [1917] AC 260.

[18] Ibid., p. 293.

[19] Constitution of India, 1950 (India) Art. 22 read together with Entry 3 of List I in the Seventh Schedule.

[20] *AK Roy v. Union of India* [1982] SCR (2) 272.

[21] Ibid, p. 275.

regarding the use of preventive detention in times of peace. For when the British frequently resorted to the power of preventive detention under various colonial legislation as a means for suppressing Indians, Indians characterized such exercise of the power during peacetime "a very heinous offence".[22]

In pursuance of the constitutional provisions concerning preventive detention, the Indian Parliament has enacted several statutes empowering the executive to exercise the power of preventive detention. These statutes include the Unlawful Activities (Prevention) Act, 1967, the Maintenance of Internal Security Act, 1971, and the National Security Act, 1980. In addition to these, the Code of Criminal Procedure (CrPc), 1973 in sect. 107 also permits the detention of an individual in order to prevent him from committing "a breach of the peace" or disturbing "the public tranquillity". State parliaments have also passed legislation concerning preventive detention. Most prominent of these include the Jammu and Kashmir Public Safety Act, 1978. These statutes have not only been used during emergency situations but also during peacetime for arbitrarily detaining those considered a threat to the government of the day. In this context, reference can first be made to the arbitrary exercise of the power of preventive detention following the proclamation of a state of emergency on 25 June 1975 on the vague ground of internal disturbance.[23] This emergency was proclaimed only 13 days after the High Court of Allahabad declared Prime Minister Indira Gandhi's election to the Parliament void due to corrupt practices.[24] Subsequently, the preventive detention powers under the Maintenance of Internal Security Act, 1971, and the temporary law concerning preventive detention, namely the Defence of India Rules, 1971, were used to stage an unparalleled crackdown on senior opposition political leaders who demanded Mrs. Gandhi's resignation as Prime Minister over the High Court's invalidation of her election to Parliament. At least 525 opposition leaders, such as Moraji Desai, Atal Bihari Vajpayee, L.K. Advani and Charan Singh, were detained within 24 hours of the proclamation of emergency.[25] Prime Minister Gandhi's own party colleagues, who had called for her to resign, were also brought within the purview of preventive detention.[26] Thus, it is evident that Mrs. Gandhi under the guise of an emergency used the power of preventive detention as an effective tool for political oppression.

Owing to the misuse of the power of preventive detention, particularly following the invocation of the emergency in June 1975, the government of the Janata Party repealed the Maintenance of Internal Security Act in 1978. However, the Unlawful Activities (Prevention) Act, 1967 and the National Security Act, 1980 continue to remain in force. These laws have continually been used by the government of day during peacetime for oppressing its critics. For instance, in the year 2018 alone, the current government of the Bharatiya Janata Party (BJP) detained approximately

---

[22] Constituent Assembly Debates, 1949 (India), Vol. IX, pp. 1505–08 (Lok Sabha Secretariat).

[23] See above n 8, p. 37.

[24] Ibid., pp. 37–38; Iyer (2000), International Commission of Jurists (1983), p. 180.

[25] Iyer (2000), p. 109.

[26] Ibid.

100,000 individuals under these preventive detention laws.[27] Furthermore, hours before formalising the decision to rob Jammu and Kashmir of its special status by repealing Article 370 of the Indian Constitution on 5 August 2019,[28] the BJP government used sect. 107 of the CrPc to preventively detain three past Chief Ministers of Jammu and Kashmir, namely, Farooq Abdullah, Omar Abdullah and Mehbooba Mufti, for a period of 6 months. When Omar Abdullah and Mehbooba Mufti's detention orders were set to expire on 5 February 2020, fresh preventive detention orders were served on them under the Jammu and Kashmir Public Safety Act, 1978 for their alleged attempts to "provoke" the population against the decision to abrogate Article 370 of the Constitution.[29] It is manifestly evident that these detention orders were preferred by the regime in an effort to prevent these politicians from mobilising support against its far-reaching decision to strip Jammu and Kashmir of its special status—a status which it enjoyed for nearly 70 years.

In Bangladesh—a nation which gained independence from Pakistan on 16 December 1971 after a brutal war of independence—the Constitution of Bangladesh, 1972 did not originally permit the exercise of the power of preventive detention under any circumstances.[30] However, the Constitution (Second Amendment) Act, which was passed on 22 September 1973, inserted provisions in the Constitution enabling the Parliament to pass laws concerning preventive detention. It should be stressed here that the Constitution of Bangladesh, as amended on 22 September 1973, does not provide any guidance as to the circumstances which can warrant the exercise of the power of preventive detention,[31] thereby allowing the executive to resort to this extraordinary power without the precondition of a state of emergency. Furthermore, the Constitution does not stipulate adequate safeguards for mitigating the harshness of the laws concerning preventive detention. For instance, the Constitution neither stipulates the maximum period for keeping a detainee in preventive custody nor prohibits detention incommunicado. Consequently, succeeding generations of executives have taken advantage of the weaknesses of permanent and temporary laws concerning preventive detention to put down anyone considered a threat to their desire of remaining in power indefinitely. For instance, during the continuance of the last proclamation of emergency in Bangladesh from 11 January 2007 to 17 December 2008, the emergency regime preventively detained as many as 929 senior political leaders of the country.[32]

The Federal Constitution of Malaysia in Article 149(1) also empowers the Parliament to enact laws permitting the executive to exercise the power of

---

[27] Sekhri   (2020),   https://www.thehindu.com/opinion/op-ed/not-fair-just-or-reasonable/article30905962.ece

[28] Pandey (2019), https://www.bbc.com/news/world-asia-india-49234708

[29] Staff Reporter, Times of India (2020), https://timesofindia.indiatimes.com/india/sc-seeks-jk-admins-response-on-plea-against-mehbooba-muftis-detention-under-psa/articleshow/74317822.cms

[30] See above n 8, p. 216.

[31] Ibid, p. 217.

[32] Bari (2017b), pp. 71–72.

preventive detention during peacetime for maintaining public order (to be discussed in detail below in 2.6). However, the Constitution does not require preventive detention laws enacted under Article 149 to stipulate effective safeguards against the possibility of abuse of the power of preventive detention. The Internal Security Act, 1960 (ISA) was the first Act passed under Article 149 of the Constitution. It was enacted to combat the armed insurgency that had been waged by the Communist Party of Malaya (CPM) since 1948. The ISA conferred wide powers of preventive detention on the executive branch of government. For instance, the ISA allowed the preventive detention of an individual for an indefinite period of time. Although the armed insurgency came to an end in 1989 following an agreement between the Malaysian Government and the CPM, the ISA was not repealed.[33] Subsequently, the ISA during its operation for nearly 52 years, became a convenient tool for the government to silence its critics. The use of the Minister's power of detention under sect. 8(1) of the ISA was often motivated by political considerations. However, such motivation was skilfully shrouded under the façade of safeguarding national security or public order.[34] The number of opposition leaders, academics and activists detained under this Act was enormous. The most prominent abuse of the powers of preventive detention under the ISA occurred during the *Operasi Lalang* (weeding operation) in 1987 when 106 persons were detained. The detainees included leaders of opposition parties, prominent human rights activists, academics, environmentalists and businessmen.[35] Although the ISA was finally repealed in 2012 through the enactment of the Security Offences (Special Measures) Act, 2012 (SOSMA), the SOSMA also authorises the exercise of the power of preventive detention. In addition to the SOSMA, the Government in 2014 and 2015 amended and extended the operation of the Prevention of Crime Act, 1959, to allow the preventive detention of individuals for a period of 2 years at a time for safeguarding national security and for preventing the commission of crime. Thus, this Act in essence permits the detention of an individual for an indefinite period of time. Subsequently, in 2015, the Parliament passed yet another preventive detention statute, namely, the Prevention of Terrorism Act, 2015 (POTA), which, as will be evident from the discussion in Sect. 4.3.4, stipulating identical provisions as the ISA and PCA.

In light of the above discussion, it is evident that in the absence of effective safeguards constraining scope of the extraordinary power of preventive detention, the power can be used to oppress political adversaries, thereby essentially turning into "political detention".[36]

---

[33] Administrative Arrangement between the Government of Malaysia and the Communist Party of Malaya Pursuant to the Agreement to terminate Hostilities, can be accessed at http://theirwords. org/media/transfer/doc/my_cpm_1989_01-2aa2b0cc70df62b0ef0b5f519d5b3065.pdf

[34] Yatim (1995), p. 369.

[35] Saravanamuttu (2008).

[36] Harding and Hatchard (1993), p. 5.

2.5 Evolution of the Power of Preventive Detention in Malaya during the British Rule

Notwithstanding the common belief that preventive detention is a "Third World phenomenon", the historical roots of the power can be traced back to the laws enacted during the British rule in the Indian Subcontinent.[37] During its rule in the Subcontinent,[38] the British enacted as many as seven laws concerning preventive detention to maintain law and order. These laws did not confine the exercise of the power of preventive detention to proclamations of emergencies. Consequently, the British used these laws as the most convenient means of crushing nationalist movement of Indians which had threatened to bring down their rule.[39]

Notwithstanding the extensive use of preventive detentions laws in the Indian Subcontinent, it is noteworthy that the British did not consider it necessary to enact such laws in the colony of Malaya—now known as the Federation of Malaysia—until the communists staged violent opposition to their rule. In response to such violence, the Colonial administration, introduced the Emergency Regulations Ordinance (ERO), 1948, which came into force on 7 July 1948. Section 3 of the ERO authorized the High Commissioner—the highest-ranking official representing the British Government in Malaya—to proclaim a state of emergency in Malaya while sect. 4(2)(6) authorized the High Commissioner to promulgate regulations for preventively detaining individuals during the continuance of an emergency. It is, therefore, evident that in marked departure from their practice in the Indian Subcontinent, the British confined the exercise of the power of preventive detention to formally declared periods of emergency in Malaya. Furthermore, the ERO stipulated certain safeguards for mitigating the harshness of the regulations concerning preventive detention. For instance, the ERO in sect. 4(3) subjected preventive detention orders passed under relevant regulation to periodic review. However, the ERO did not stipulate the maximum period for keeping an individual in preventive custody. This is evident from the fact that while the ERO stipulated that any detention order passed in pursuance of a regulation providing for preventive detention could not exceed beyond 2 years, such detention could nevertheless be extended by a further order.[40]

On 12 July 1948—5 days after the coming into force of the ERO—the High Commissioner in exercise of its power under sect. 3 of the ERO declared a state of

---

[37] Ibid., pp. 2–5; See above n 8, p. 97.

[38] The British rule in the Subcontinent can be divided into informal and formal rule. The informal rule of the British refers to the rule of the East India Company in the Subcontinent from 1765 to 1858. Subsequently, the Royal Proclamation of Queen Victoria issued on 1 November 1858 under the Government of India Act, 1858 dissolved the East India Company and this in turn marked the beginning of the formal British rule in India.

[39] Ashutosh (2014), p. 24.

[40] Emergency Regulations Ordinance, 1948 - Federation of Malaya Ordinance No. X of 1948, Section 4(3)(a).

emergency to tide over the threats posed by the communists. Subsequently, on 15 July 1948, the High Commissioner promulgated the Emergency Regulations, 1948, which in Regulation 17 authorized the Chief Secretary of Malaya to:

> direct [by an order] that any person named in such order shall be detained for any period not exceeding one year in such place of detention as may be specified by the Chief Secretary in the order.

It is evident from the above provision that notwithstanding the provision contained in sect. 4(3)(a), the Emergency Regulations, 1948 stipulated a maximum period of 1 year for keeping an individual in preventive custody. Furthermore, under the Regulations, detainees could make representations against their orders of detention before an "Advisory Committee", which could in turn make recommendations to the High Commissioner regarding the fate of detainees on the basis of the representations.[41]

Within hours of the promulgation of the Regulations of 1948, the law enforcement agencies, according to one estimation, detained approximately 1000 CPM members or supporters.[42] It is striking that by the end of the year 1948, the authorities had preventively detained 11,779 individuals.[43] The number of detainees rose to 33,992 by 31 August 1957 when Malaysia emerged as an independent nation.[44]

It is evident from the above discussion that the power of preventive detention originated in the Indian Subcontinent at the behest of the British to subvert the Indian Nationalist Movement. The power was, subsequently, introduced by the British to the land now known as Malaysia in 1948 to deter communist insurgents who posed a violent threat to the security of the Federation. However, in stark contrast to its practice of not confining the exercise of the power of preventive detention to declared periods of emergency in the Indian Subcontinent, the British limited the exercise of such power in Malaya to genuine emergencies.

2.6 The Constitution of Malaysia and the Provisions Concerning Preventive Detention

Following Malaysia's emergence as an independent nation on 31 August 1957 under the leadership of an Alliance Government consisting of three ethnic-based political parties, which had won office in the elections held in 1955, a constitutional commission comprising of five distinguished jurists—two from Britain and one each from Australia, India and Pakistan—completed the task of drafting a Constitution for Malaysia. The practice of entrusting an expert body devoid of any representation of the locals stands in contradistinction to the practice followed in other independent

---

[41] Emergency Regulations 1948 - Federation of Malaya Ordinance No. X of 1948, paras 2, 3 and 4.
[42] Munir (1993), p. 132.
[43] Ibid.
[44] Ibid.

nations of the Commonwealth, such as India and Pakistan. For both in India and Pakistan, Constituent Assemblies—composed of elected representatives—carried out the pivotal task of framing the Constitution for their respective nations. However, the head of the Alliance Government—Tunku Abdul Rahman—was of the opinion that the locals were not suitably qualified for the task of drafting a Constitution for the newly independent nation and, as such, he deemed it fit "to invite persons with specialised knowledge of constitutions of federal government" to carry out such task.[45]

The Federation of Malaya Constitutional Commission (popularly known as the Reid Commission as it was chaired by Lord Reid) embarked on the journey of drafting the Constitution at a time when the Federation of Malaya was under a state of emergency proclaimed by the Colonial Government in July 1948 to put down the communist insurgency. The gravity of the threat posed to the organised life of the nation by the insurgents persuaded the Reid Commission to reach the conclusion that the newly independent nation required special powers against subversion in the Constitution, as is evident from the following observations contained in the Report of the Commission:

> To deal with any further attempt by any substantial body of persons to organise violence against persons or property, by a majority we recommend that Parliament should be authorised to enact provisions designed for the purpose notwithstanding that such provisions may involve infringements of fundamental rights or State rights. It must be for the Parliament to determine whether the situation is such that special provisions are required but Parliament should not be entitled to authorise infringement of such a character that they cannot properly be regarded as designed to deal with the particular situation. It would be open to any person aggrieved by the enactment of a particular infringement to maintain that it could not properly be so regarded and to submit the question for decision by the Court. We see no need to recommend that the executive should have any emergency powers to act in such a situation before Parliament has enacted legislation to deal with it.[46]

Accordingly, the Reid Commission not only suggested the insertion of provisions concerning the proclamation of emergency but also provisions authorising the exercise of the power of preventive detention in the Federal Constitution of Malaysia. Article 150(1) of the Malaysian Constitution originally authorised the executive branch of government to proclaim an emergency when "the security, or the economic life, or public order in the Federation or any part thereof …[was] threatened whether by war or external aggression or internal disturbance".[47] It seems that the

---

[45] Memorandum by Tunku Abdul Rahman, 1 March 1955, Malayan Chinese Association Files, MCA Headquarters, Kuala Lumpur, PH/A/0084.

[46] Federation of Malaya Constitutional Commission (1957), Chap. IX Fundamental Rights—Emergency Powers, para174.

[47] The Malaysian Constitution was amended in 1963 to substantially widen the scope of the power of the executive to proclaim a state of emergency. For the Amendment Act, 1963 substantially widened the scope of the power of the executive branch of government to proclaim a state of emergency by deleting the words "war or external aggression or internal disturbance" as grounds for invoking such an emergency. Thus, the executive is now empowered to proclaim an emergency without the precondition of the security or economy of the nation being threatened by war or exter-

grounds for declaring emergency of war, external aggression and internal disturbance were reproduced from the original provisions of Article 352(1) of the
Constitution of India, 1950.[48] Furthermore, clause 2 of Article 150 of the Constitution
originally empowered the executive to invoke a state of emergency even before the
actual occurrence of war or external aggression or internal disturbance. This provision authorising the executive to proclaim an emergency even before the actual
occurrence of an emergency is also reproduced from the original clause 3 of Article
352 of the Indian Constitution.[49]

While Article 149(1) of the Constitution originally provided that

> If an Act of Parliament recites that action has been taken or threatened by any substantial
> body of persons, whether inside or outside the Federation, to cause, or to cause a substantial
> number of citizens to fear, organized violence against persons or property, any provision of
> that law designed to stop or prevent that action is valid notwithstanding that it is inconsis-
> tent with any of the provisions of Article 5, 9, or 10, or would apart from this Article be
> outside the legislative power of Parliament;

Thus, it is evident that the above enabling provision does not confine the exercise
of preventive detention to only emergencies declared in pursuance of Article 150 of
the Federal Constitution of Malaysia. In this context, the dissenting observations of
one of the eminent members of the Commission, namely, Justice Abdul Hamid—
then a Judge of the West Pakistan High Court—regarding the issue of authorizing
the exercise of the power of preventive detention without the precondition of an
emergency as warranted by Article 149 of the Constitution, are noteworthy:

> If there arises any real emergency, and that should only be an emergency of the type men-
> tioned in [Article 150], then and only then should such extraordinary powers be exercised.
> It is ... unsafe to leave in the hands of the Parliament power to suspend constitutional guar-
> antees only by making a recital in the preamble that conditions in the country are beyond
> the reach of the ordinary law. Ordinary legislation and executive measures are enough to
> cope with a situation of the type described in [Article 149]. That article should be ... omit-
> ted. There should be no half-way house between government by ordinary legislation and
> government by extraordinary legislation.[50]

---

nal aggression or internal disturbance. The Malaysian emergency provisions, as amended in 1963,
are one of the classic examples of permitting "broadest grants of emergency powers to the executive" as it in essence enables the executive to invoke an emergency for extraneous purposes, such
as putting down protests against unpopular policies of the government of the day. Martinez
(2005–06), p. 2496.

[48] Article 352(1) of the Constitution of India, 1950 (India) originally empowered the President to
proclaim an emergency when "the security of India or of any part of the territory thereof... [was]
threatened, whether by war or external aggression or internal disturbance". However, Section 37 of
the Constitution (Forty-Fourth Amendment) Act, 1978 (India) replaced "internal disturbance" with
"armed rebellion" as one of the grounds for invoking an emergency.

[49] Article 352(3) of the Constitution of India, 1950 (India) originally empowered the President to
proclaim an emergency in anticipation of an emergency threatening the security of the nation by
war or external aggression or internal disturbance.

[50] Note of Dissent by Mr. Justice Abdul Hamid, para 13 (vii), Report of the Federation of Malaya
Constitutional Commission 1957.

It seems that Justice Hamid expressed the above words of caution in light of the disturbing use of the power of preventive detention by the British in the Subcontinent in times of peace for suppressing nationalist movement of Indians. Notwithstanding these cautionary words, the special power of the Parliament to enact laws concerning preventive detention without the precondition of a state of emergency found a place in Article 149 of the Federal Constitution, 1957. To this end, it seems the majority of the members of the Commission were influenced by the Indian Constitution, which, as pointed out earlier in Sect. 2.4, also permits the exercise of the power of preventive detention during peacetime.[51]

Thus, the Parliament by virtue of Article 149 has been made the sole judge to determine whether any given situation warrants the enactment of a statute concerning preventive detention. However, Article 149 of the Constitution in its current form does not contain the same features of the original provision as it has been amended on a number of occasions since 1957.

2.6.1   Amendments to Article 149 of the Federal Constitution

Article 149, which authorises the exercise of the power of preventive detention during peacetime, is contained in Part XI of the Federal Constitution. The heading of Part XI of the Constitution was originally titled "Special Powers Against Subversion and Emergency Powers" and Article 149 was originally titled "Legislation against subversion". Article 149(1) of the Constitution, as discussed above in 2.6, originally empowered the Parliament to enact legislation to deal with actions which "cause a substantial number of citizens to fear, organized violence against persons or property". The provision contained in Article 149(1) further stated that such legislation would be considered valid notwithstanding its inconsistency with other provisions of the Constitution, namely: (a) Article 5—guaranteeing the liberty of the person; (b) Article 9—guaranteeing the prohibition of banishment and freedom of movement; and (c) Article 10—guaranteeing freedom of speech, assembly and association. Furthermore, clause (2) of Article 149 originally imposed a time limit on the continuation of a statute providing for preventive detention. For it stated that any statue enacted under clause (1) of Article 149, if not repealed earlier, would "cease to have effect on the expiration of a period of one year from the date on which it came into operation". However, Article 149 has undergone a number of changes through constitutional amendments introduced in 1960, 1978 and 1981 respectively. An attempt will now be made to discuss in detail the changes introduced by these three Amendments Acts.

---

[51] Constitution of India, 1950 (India) Art. 22 read together with Entry 3 of List I in the Seventh Schedule.

2.6.1.1   The Changes Introduced by the Constitution (Amendment) Act, 1960

The Constitution (Amendment) Act of 1960 substituted clause (1) of Article 149 with a new one, which substantially broadened the authority of the Parliament to enact laws concerning preventive detention. Article 149(1), as amended by the Amendment Act of 1960, stipulated that a preventive detention statute enacted by the Parliament should contain a recital to the effect that it had been enacted for dealing with one of the following consequences stipulated by Article 149(1):

(a) to cause, or to cause a substantial number of citizens to fear, organized violence against persons or property; or
(b) to excite disaffection against the Yang di-Pertuan Agong or any Government in the Federation; or
(c) to promote feelings of ill-will and hostility between different races or other classes of the population likely to cause violence; or
(d) to procure the alteration, otherwise than by lawful means, of anything by law established; or
(e) which is prejudicial to the security of the Federation or any part thereof.[52]

Furthermore, the amendment of 1960 retained the second part of the original clause 1 of Article 149, which asserted the validity of preventive detention laws notwithstanding their inconsistency with the fundamental rights guaranteed by Articles 5, 9 and 10 of the Constitution, as the proviso to amended clause 1. But the amendment substituted clause (2) of Article 149 with a new one, which states that a statute passed under clause (1), if not repealed earlier, shall "cease to have effect if resolutions are passed by both Houses of Parliament annulling such law". Thus, by virtue of the amendment of 1960, preventive laws passed under Article 149(1) can remain in force for an indefinite period of time and consequently, become permanent features of the legal system.

2.6.1.2   The Constitution (Amendment) Act, 1978

In 1978, the Malaysian Parliament passed the Constitution (Amendment) Act, 1978, which, in the first place, renamed the heading of Part XI of the Constitution. The new heading reads: "SPECIAL POWERS AGAINST SUBVERSION, ORGANISED VIOLENCE, AND ACTS AND CRIMES PREJUDICIAL TO THE PUBLIC AND EMERGENCY POWERS". The Amendment Act also altered the title of Article 149 by inserting the words "action prejudicial to public order, etc" after the word "subversion" in the title.

Moreover, two new changes were introduced to Article 149(1) by this Amendment Act of 1948. Paragraph (e) of clause (1) of Article 149 was substituted with a new one, which warrants the exercise of the power of preventive detention for preventing

---

[52] Constitution (Amendment) Act, 1960 (Malaysia) Sec. 28.

the commission of an act "which is prejudicial to the maintenance or the functioning of any supply or service to the pubic or any class of the public in the Federation or any part thereof".[53] While a new paragraph (f) was added to clause 1 of Article 149 authorising the enactment of an Act to prevent or stop an action "which is prejudicial to public order in, or the security of, the Federation or any part thereof".[54]

2.6.1.3   The Constitution (Amendment) Act, 1981

Article 149 of the Constitution, as pointed out earlier in Sects. 2.6.1 and 2.6.1.2, originally asserted the legitimacy of preventive detention laws notwithstanding their inconsistency with the rights guaranteed by Articles 5, 9 and 10. In 1981, the Parliament passed yet another Constitutional (Amendment) Act proclaiming the validity of preventive detention laws against fundamental liberty, namely the right to property guaranteed by Article 13 of the Constitution.[55] Thus, Article 149(1) as it stands now stipulates that the validity of any preventive detention law passed by the Parliament cannot be questioned on account of their inconsistencies with the fundamental rights guaranteed by Articles 5, 9, 10 or 13 of the Constitution.

In light of the above discussion, it is evident that the amendments introduced to Article 149 of the Constitution over the years have significantly broadened the scope of the power of the Parliament to enact preventive detention laws on a wide-ranging grounds and to deprive citizens a number of fundamental rights of citizens without the precondition of a state of emergency.

An attempt will now be made to critically evaluate current provisions of Article 149 of the Federal Constitution.

2.6.2   Critical Evaluation of Article 149 of the Federal Constitution

By virtue of Article 149, which is a provision under Part XI, titled "Special Powers Against Subversion, Organized Violence, And Acts And Crimes Prejudicial To The Public And Emergency Powers" of the Federal Constitution of Malaysia, the Parliament is vested with the power to enact preventive detention laws during peacetime. Once subversion of any kind has occurred, Article 149 of the Constitution enables the Parliament to make laws empowering the executive to take measures not only for suppressing it but also for preventing its recurrence.[56] The only precondition to the enactment of a statute in pursuance of Article 149 is that the Act must

---

[53] Section 5 of the Constitution (Amendment) Act, 1978.

[54] Ibid.

[55] Section 14 of the Constitution (Amendment) Act 1981.

[56] *Teh Cheng Poh v. Public Prosecutor* [1979] 1 MLJ 50, 54 (per Lord Diplock).

have a recital stating that "an action has been taken or threatened by any substantial body of persons whether inside or outside the Federation" and that the action that has been taken or threatened causes one of the following consequences stipulated by Article 149(1):

  (a) to cause, or to cause a substantial number of citizens to fear, organized violence against persons or property; or
  (b) to excite disaffection against the yang di-pertuan Agong or any Government in the Federation; or
  (c) to promote feelings of ill-will and hostility between different races or other classes of the population likely to cause violence; or
  (d) to procure the alteration, otherwise than by lawful means, of anything by law established; or
  (e) which is prejudicial to the maintenance or the functioning of any supply or service to the public or any class of the public in the Federation or any part thereof; or
  (f) which is prejudicial to public order in, or the security of, the Federation or any part thereof,

The effect of Article 149 is that an Act of Parliament containing the necessary recital cannot be held invalid on any ground.[57] Accordingly, preventive detention legislation in Malaysia have contained recitals, which are identical to the wordings specified in Article 149. For instance, the Internal Security Act (ISA), 1960 in its recital incorporated the first sentence of Article 149(1), i.e. "[w]hereas action has been ...", and subsequently included paragraphs (a) and (d) of clause 1 of this Article. Similarly the Security Offences (Special Measures) Act, 2012 (SOSMA) in its recital contains the first sentence of clause 1 of Article 149 and also paragraphs (a), (b), (d) and (f) of clause 1, and the Preventive of Crime Act, 1959 (PCA), as amended in 2014 and 2015, has only included paragraph (a) of Article 149(1) in its recital along with the first sentence of clause 1. In the same vein, the Prevention of Terrorism Act, 2015 (POTA) has incorporated the first sentence of Article 149(1) and the second part of paragraph (f) of clause 1.[58]

It seems that if the question arises in a court of law as to whether there existed any of the circumstances mentioned in the recital of an Act passed in pursuance of Article 149 then the court is merely required to be satisfied that the Act in question contains the recital as required by Article 149. The court would not go beyond the recital to decide whether it was necessary to enact the Act in question.[59] This is evident from the enactment of the ISA, SOSMA, PCA and POTA in 1960, 2012, 2014 and 2015 respectively.

Moreover, a close scrutiny of Article 149 of the Federal Constitution reveals that this constitutional provision is characterized by subjective terms, such as "substantial body", "substantial number", "cause to fear", 'excite disaffection', "promote feelings of ill will and hostility". All these terms embody wide areas of discretionary interpretation. The Parliament is not required to define the activities that are subversive or prejudicial to the security of the nation which urged them to enact

---

[57] L.A. Sheridan (1961), p. 562.

[58] The POTA's recital states that: 'WHEREAS action has been taken and further action is threatened by a substantial body of persons both inside and outside Malaysia which is prejudicial to the security of Malaysia or any part of Malaysia.'

[59] Jayakumar (1978), pp. 9–24.

such legislation during peace time by virtue of Article 149 of the Constitution. It is, therefore, for the executive authority or any particular body authorized under the preventive detention statute to determine whether any particular activity of an individual is prejudicial to national security, thereby bringing him within the purview of the preventive detention statute.

This special power provided under Article 149 is susceptible to abuse as anything and everything can fall within the purview of the actions which will result in the consequences stipulated by the provisions of this Article and empower the relevant authorities[60] to detain a person. Furthermore, it will be demonstrated in this Book that by bestowing such extraordinary power directly or indirectly on the executive through these statutes clearly provides the government of the day with the opportunity to stifle legitimate dissent by putting political adversaries behind the bars for an indefinite period of time. In this context, the observations of a British Politician, Herbert Morrison, are worth quoting. For he warned about the dangers of warranting the exercise of the power of preventive detention during peacetime while commenting on the application of the British Defence Regulations, which permitted the exercise of preventive detention during peacetime, in the following manner:

> I am not going to use the argument usually put forward as a matter of courtesy that we do not believe the present Minister would be wicked but that we are afraid his successors might be. I think that any Minister is capable of being wicked when he has a body of regulations like this to administer.[61]

2.6.3   The Constitutional Safeguards against the Abuse of the Power of Preventive Detention

The Constitution being the supreme law of a nation is the best possible means of stipulating adequate safeguards against the abuse of the power of preventive detention. Accordingly, the Reid Commission in its Report recommended the insertion of certain safeguards in the Constitution for mitigating the harshness of the extraordinary power of preventive detention. The following analysis will seek to explore whether the safeguards stipulated by Articles 149 and 151 of the Malaysian Constitution are adequate for preventing abuse of this extraordinary power.

(a) **Indefinite Continuation of the Preventive Detention Laws**

The original Article 149(2), as discussed earlier in Sect. 2.6, stipulated a maximum time limit of 1 year on the continuation of a law concerning preventive detention. But through a subsequent amendment, namely the Constitution Amendment

---

[60] The relevant authorities under sections 8 and 73 of the ISA were the Home Minister or the police force. The SOSMA, in following in the footsteps of the ISA, has empowered the same authorities under sect. 4 while a particular body has been empowered under section 19A of the PCA and sect. 13 of the POTA.

[61] Quoted in Aldred and Wynn (2012), p. 25.

Act 1960, this clause was replaced with one which stipulates that a law enacted under Article 149 can continue to be in force, if not repealed earlier, until resolutions are passed by both Houses of the Parliament annulling such law. Thus, any Act passed under this Article can continue to remain in force for an indefinite period. This argument is bolstered by the continuation of the ISA for almost 52 years.

(b) Curtailment of the Fundamental Liberties under Article 5

The Constitution of Malaysia guarantees nine fundamental liberties to individuals and among these is the "liberty of the person", which finds expression in Article 5. In addition to guaranteeing the right to liberty, Article 5 affords certain safeguards to individuals who are deprived of their liberty "in accordance with law". These safeguards can be summarized as follows:

(i) the High Court has the authority to examine the legality of one's detention order in pursuance of a writ of *habeas corpus* (Clause 2);
(ii) a detainee should be informed of the grounds of detention "as soon as may be" (Clause 3);
(iii) a detainee has been afforded the right to consult and to be defended by a legal practitioner of one's choice (Clause 3);
(iv) a detainee should be produced before a Magistrate within 24 hour of his/her detention and should not be further detained without the Magistrate's authority (Clause 4). Although these safeguards are available to individuals detained under the laws passed by virtue of Article 149 of the Constitution, the proviso to clause 4 of Article 5 of the Constitution specifically excludes the extension of these safeguards to any person arrested or detained under any law relating to restricted residence.

However, rather than only permitting the curtailment of the right to liberty of individuals by the exercise of the power of preventive detention during a state of emergency under Article 150, the Constitution also allows the exercise of this extraordinary power under Article 149 during peacetime. Furthermore, the proviso to Article 149 of the Constitution, as pointed out earlier in Sect. 2.6.1.3, validates any preventive detention law regardless of its inconsistencies with the liberties guaranteed by Articles 5 (liberty of the person), 9 (prohibition of banishment and freedom of movement), 10 (freedom of speech, assembly and association) and 13 (right to property). This essentially means that anyone deprived of his liberty under any preventive detention law passed in pursuance of Article 149 will simultaneously be deprived of the safeguards stipulated by Article 5 of the Constitution, which are designed to further strengthen the guarantee contained therein. Consequently, the preventive detention laws passed by the Malaysian Parliament, namely the ISA, PCA and POTA, have contained provisions that deprive the detainees of the above safeguards, such as the right to challenge the legality of a detention order in pursuance of a writ of *habeas corpus* on substantive grounds, the right to consult and to be defended by a legal practitioner.

It is pertinent to note here that it is not an uncommon practice for the constitutions of some of the other new polities in the Commonwealth to deprive individuals of some of the above safeguards under preventive detention laws. For instance, the Constitution India, in the first place, also authorizes the enactment of laws which warrant the exercise of the power of preventive detention during peacetime. It further stipulates in Article 22 that the safeguards, such as the obligation of the detaining authority to: (a) furnish 'as soon as possible' to the detainee the grounds of his arrest; (b) allow the detainee to consult and to be defended by a lawyer,[62] and (c) produce the detainee before a Magistrate within 24 hour of his arrest and the prohibition on detaining him beyond the said period,[63] which are afforded to an arrested individual shall not apply to any person who is "detained under any law providing for preventive detention".[64] In Pakistan, Article 10(1)[65] and (2)[66] of the Constitution of the Islamic Republic of Pakistan, 1973, affords similar safeguards to an individual arrested and detained under the ordinary criminal justice system while Clause (3) of Article 10 specifically stipulates that these safeguards shall not "apply to any person who is arrested or detained under any law providing for preventive detention". However, it should be stressed here that neither of these Constitutions exclude the authority of their respective judiciaries to examine the legality of the preventive detention orders in pursuance of writs of *habeas corpus*.

Therefore, the Constitutional deprivation of the authority of the judiciary to examine the lawfulness of preventive detention orders is a unique "departure from the normal constitutional pattern followed elsewhere".[67] This in turn has the adverse impact of undermining the authority of the Malaysian judiciary to act as the protector and guarantor of the fundamental liberties guaranteed by the Constitution by preventing executive attempt to arbitrarily interfere with their enjoyment. In this context, the observations of the High Court Division of the Supreme Court of

---

[62] Constitution of India, 1950 (India) Art. 22(1)—No person who is arrested shall be detained in custody without being informed, as soon as may be, of the grounds for such arrest nor shall he be denied the right to consult, and to be defended by, a legal practitioner of his choice.

[63] Constitution of India 1950 (India) Art. 22(2)—Every person who is arrested and detained in custody shall be produced before the nearest magistrate within a period of 24 h of such arrest excluding the time necessary for the journey from the place of arrest to the court of the magistrate and no such person shall be detained in custody beyond the said period without the authority of a magistrate.

[64] Constitution of India 1950 (India) Art. 22(3)(b).

[65] Constitution of Islamic Republic of Pakistan, 1973 (Pakistan) Art. 10(1)—No person who is arrested shall be detained in custody without being informed, as soon as may be, of the grounds for such arrest, nor shall he be denied the right to consult and be defended by a legal practitioner of his choice.

[66] Constitution of Islamic Republic of Pakistan, 1973 (Pakistan) Art. 10(2)—Every person who is arrested and detained in custody shall be produced before a magistrate within a period of 24 h of such arrest, excluding the time necessary for the journey from the place of arrest to the court of the nearest magistrate, and no such person shall be detained in custody beyond the said period without the authority of a magistrate.

[67] F. K. M. A. Munim (1975), p. 333 quoted in Bari (2017), p. 202.

Bangladesh in the case of *Aruna Sen v Government of Bangladesh*[68] is worthy of quote:

> [T]he well settled principle of law endorsed by a long line of judicial authorities [is that] … any person charged with the authority of taking decisions affecting the rights and liberties of the citizens of the State has the corresponding duty of acting judicially and the superior courts having supervisory jurisdiction over such person have the power to see whether the said person conformed to the judicial norms applicable to the case.[69]

(c) **Procedural Safeguards under Article 151**

Article 151, titled "Restrictions on Preventive Detention", of the Federal Constitution provides certain procedural safeguards to the persons detained under the laws enacted in pursuance of Articles 149 and 150 of the Constitution. In the case of *Kandupillai Krishnan v Timbalan Menteri Dalam Negeri, Malaysia & Ors*,[70] the High Court held that "Article 151 of the Federal Constitution accords certain minimum protection to protect detainees against possible abuse of the wide powers of preventive detention under legislation enacted pursuant to arts 149 and 150".[71] The procedural safeguards afforded by Article 151(1) [72] can be summarized as follows: (1) communication to the detainee of his grounds of detention; and (2) right of the detainee to make a representation against the detention order before an Advisory Board.

Rather than stipulating a specific time-frame within which the above safeguards should be made available to an individual kept in preventive custody, the Constitution of Malaysia in Article 151(1)(a) has kept the time limit for communicating the grounds of detention to the detainee indeterminate through the use of the imprecise expression "as soon as may be". Since the communication of the grounds of detention in clear and unambiguous terms is essential for an effective representation by the detainee against the detention order, it is evident that the Constitution has significantly weakened the effectiveness of such a representation by providing the detaining authority broad power to withhold the communication of the grounds of detention and allegations of fact for an indefinite period of time. In this context, the observations of Chief Justice Kania of the Supreme Court of India in the case of *State of Bombay v Atma Ram Shridhar Vaidya*[73] are pertinent. As he observed:

---

[68] *Aruna Sen v Government of* [1974] 3 CLC (HCD) 1.

[69] Ibid., p. 8.

[70] *Bangladesh Kandupillai Krishnan v Timbalan Menteri Dalam Negeri, Malaysia & Ors* [2004] 1 MLJ 85.

[71] Ibid., para 54.

[72] Federal Constitution of Malaysia, 1957 (Malaysia) Art. 151(1)(a) - Where any law or ordinance made or promulgated in pursuance of this Part provides for preventive detention—(a) the authority on whose order any person is detained under that law or ordinance shall, as soon as may be, inform him of the grounds for his detention and, subject to Clause (3), the allegations of fact on which the order is based, and shall give him the opportunity of making representations against the order as soon as may be.

[73] *State of Bombay v Atma Ram Shridhar Vaidya* A.I.R. 1951 S.C. 157.

[I]f the representation has to be intelligible to meet the charges contained in the grounds, the information conveyed to the detained person must be sufficient to attain that objective ... Without getting information sufficient to make a representation against the order of deten- tion, it is not possible for the man to make the representation. Indeed, the right will be only illusory but not a real right at all.[74]

Article 151(1)(b) of the Constitution originally required the Advisory Board- a quasi-judicial body- to consider the representation of the detainee within 3 months from the date of detention, which in turn provided some degree of certainty to the detainee with respect to the timeframe within which he would be allowed to make a representation against his detention order. But this requirement has been changed through the Constitution Amendment Acts of 1960[75] and 1976[76] so as to do away with the time limit within which an advisory board was required to consider repre- sentation from the detainee, thereby casting further doubt on the effectiveness of this safeguard.

As to the composition of the Advisory Board, Article 151(2), which has under- gone a number of amendments in line with the changes to the judicial structure of the country,[77] stipulates that such a Board should be consisted of three members, namely one chairman and two members. The Yang di-Pertuan Agong (YDPA) shall appoint the Chairman who "shall be or have been or qualified to be a judge of

---

[74] Ibid., pp. 161–162.

[75] Federal Constitution of Malaysia, 1957 (Malaysia) Art. 151(1)(b), as amended by Sec. 30, Act 10 of 1960, provided that—"No citizen shall be detained under that law or ordinance for a period exceeding 3 months unless an advisory board constituted as mentioned in Clause (2) has consid- ered any representations made by him under paragraph (a) and made recommendations thereon to the Yang di Pertuan Agong'.

[76] Federal Constitution of Malaysia, 1957 (Malaysia) Art. 151(1)(b), as amended by Sec. 40 of Act 354 of 1976, provides that "No citizen shall continue to be detained under that law or ordinance unless an advisory board constituted as mentioned in Clause (2) has considered any representa- tions made by him under paragraph *(a)* and made recommendations thereon to the Yang di-Pertuan Agong within 3 months of receiving such representations, or within such longer period as the Yang di-Pertuan Agong may allow".

[77] When Malaysia emerged as an independent nation, the Supreme Court was the highest court sit- ting below the Privy Council. However, when the Federation of Malaysia was established in September 1963, Part IX of the Constitution was amended to alter the structure of the superior judiciary. Following the restructure: a) a newly established Federal Court replaced the Supreme Court as the apex court of law in Malaysia; and b) three High Courts were established. Twenty years later in 1983, another constitutional amendment was introduced establishing the Supreme Court as the final court of appeal and the highest court of the land. For all provisions of the Constitution, which authorized appeals from Malaysia to the Privy Council, were abolished. Thus, following this latest amendment, a two-tier superior court system came into effect in Malaysia- a) the Supreme Court as the final court of appeal in Malaysia and b) the two High Courts- one for Peninsular Malaysia and the other for Borneo.
Finally, 11 years later on 24 June 1994, the Constitution (Amendment) Act, 1994 was passed to: (a) rename the Supreme Court as the Federal Court; and (b) establish a Court of Appeal. Thus, Malaysia currently has a three-tier superior court system, namely: (a) the Federal Court as the highest court of the nation; (b) the Court of Appeal as an intermediary court between the Federal Court and the two High Courts; and c) two High Courts- one for Malaya and the other for Sabah and Sarawak. See Bari (2011), pp. 53–54.

the-Federal Court or the Court of Appeal or the High Court or before Malaysia Day of the Supreme Court".[78] The two other members shall also be appointed by the YDPA but the Constitution does not prescribe any guideline or criteria for their appointment. Article 151(2), before the amendment of 1990, required the YDPA to appoint these members after consulting the Lord President of the Supreme Court. But after the changes made by the Constitution (Amendment) Act of 1990,[79] Article 151(2) does not contain any similar requirements of consultation by the YDPA. This leaves the door wide open for favourites or loyalists of the regime to be appointed as members of the Board, who in turn can hardly be expected to be objective in putting forward their recommendations.

However, the Constitution does not empower the Advisory Board constituted under Article 151 of the Federal Constitution to free those it determines to have been wrongly detained.[80] Instead the Board can only make non-binding recommendations to the YDPA. But in this context, it is necessary to shed light on the provisions of Article 40(1A) of the Constitution. For its states that

> In the exercise of his functions under this Constitution or federal law, where the Yang di-Pertuan Agong is to act in accordance with advice, on advice, or after considering advice, the Yang di-Pertuan Agong shall accept and act in accordance with such advice.

A close perusal of this provision reveals that the Constitution itself makes it mandatory, by the use of the word "shall", for the YDPA to accept an advice and to act in accordance with it. However, practice shows otherwise. The Advisory Board's recommendations for the release of individuals detained under the repealed ISA were often ignored. For instance, in November and December 2002, the Board recommended the release of five *Parti Keadilan Rakyat* (the Peoples' Justice Party) activists, namely, Tian Chua, Saar, Sungrib, Likman Noor Adam, Badrulamin Bahron and Hishamuddin Rais.[81] But the YDPA did not pay attention to these recommendations.[82] In this context, the opinion of P. Ramakrishnan, the head of the civil society group, ALIRAN, is noteworthy:

> If the government cannot honour the decision of the Advisory Board, if it continues to show scant respect to the rule of law, then what is the point in having the Advisory Board? What purpose is served in going through this charade? Let's scrap this meaningless and perverse

---

[78] Federal Constitution of Malaysia, 1957 (Malaysia) Art. 151(2).

[79] Federal Constitution of Malaysia, 1957 (Malaysia) Art. 151(2) as amended by sec. 5 of Act A767, on May 11, 1990 read as follows:

> (2) An advisory board constituted for the purposes of this Article shall consist of a chairman, who shall be appointed by the yang di-pertuan Agong and who shall be or have been, or be qualified to be, a judge of the Supreme Court or a high Court, or shall before Malaysia Day have been a judge of the Supreme Court, and two other members, who shall be appointed by the yang di-pertuan Agong after consultation with the Lord president of the Supreme Court.

[80] Human Rights Watch (2004), p. 39, https://www.hrw.org/reports/2004/malaysia0504/malaysia0504.pdf

[81] Ibid., p. 40.

[82] Ramakrishnan (2003). Available at http://aliran.com/archives/ms/2003/0115.html

provision. The Advisory Board comes across as nothing more than a farcical facade of democracy which makes a mockery of justice.[83]

Finally, it should be stressed here that the procedural safeguards prescribed, as discussed earlier, by Article 151(1) of the Constitution are further weakened by clause 3 of Article 151, which gives wide discretion to the detaining authority to withhold the grounds of detention if in its estimation disclosure is considered to be against the national interest. It seems that this provision for withholding the grounds of detention is reproduced from Article 352(6) of the Constitution of India, 1950. For Article 352(6) of the Indian Constitution also authorises the detaining authority to refrain from disclosing the grounds of detention if such disclosure is considered "to be against the public interest".

(d) **Indefinite Period of Preventive Detention**

Neither Article 5 nor Article 149 of the Malaysian Constitution has specified the time frame for which a person may be deprived of his personal liberty for the maintenance of national security and public order. In this context, the constitutional arrangement in Pakistan—a nation which like Malaysia also allows for preventive—is noteworthy. The 1973 Constitution of Pakistan in Article 10(7) specifies that no individual can be detained "for more than a total period of eight months in the case of a person detained for acting in a manner prejudicial to public order and twelve months in any other case". Thus, the Constitution of Pakistan provides the most significant safeguard to an individual kept in preventive custody by prescribing the maximum period of detention.

However, instead of stipulating a maximum time period for keeping a detainee in preventive custody, it seems the Malaysian Constitution has followed in the footsteps of the Indian Constitution of 1950. For Article 22 of the Constitution of India also endows the Parliament with the absolute authority to specify by law the maximum time limit on the continuation of a preventive detention order.

(e) **Detention Incommunicado**

Detention incommunicado refers to detention without: (a) publishing the name of the detainee, (b) allowing the detainee of the opportunity to approach a court or to consult a lawyer, and (c) permitting the detainee to meet with family members.[84] Consequently, it can be argued that detention of this nature enables detaining authorities to resort to extreme measures, such as torturing the detainee, without having to worry that the outside world will be privy to information concerning such abuse. Therefore, in order to obviate the possibility of such grave abuse, an individual kept in preventive custody should not be denied access to the outside world. In this context, the guarantee offered by the Constitution of South Africa is noteworthy. Section 37(6)(b) imposes an obligation on the detaining authority to publish a notice in the national Government Gazette within 5 days of the detention of an

---

[83] Ibid.
[84] See above n 32, p. 7.

individual, "stating the detainee's name and place of detention and referring to the emergency measure in terms of which that person has been detained". However, a safeguard of this nature has not found a place in the Constitution of Malaysia and as a result the detainees are kept in unknown detention centers. For instance, recently Maria Chin Abdullah, a leading human rights activist and Chairperson of the electoral reform group—*Bersih* 2.0—was arrested and detained incommunicado under the SOSMA for the initial 48 hours of her detention.[85] According to her lawyers and family members, she was kept in "solitary confinement in a 2.5 m x 4.5 m cell without a window or proper ventilation".[86]

It is noteworthy that in addition to the guarantee, as mentioned above, against detention incommunicado, the Constitution of South Africa also confers three other guarantees against detention incommunicado, namely, the requirement of a family member or friend of the detainee to be communicated about the detention, the right to choose and be visited by a medical practitioner and legal practitioner within a reasonable period of time. Although the Constitution of Malaysia provides the right to be defended by a lawyer in Article 5, the security laws, namely the PCA[87] and POTA,[88] specifically mentions that this right is not available to the detainee who is deprived of his liberty during the inquiry stage "except when his own evidence is being taken and recorded by the Inquiry Officer". Furthermore, both the POTA and the PCA neither requires the presence of the detainee who is the subject of the inquiry nor his lawyer before the Prevention of Terrorism Board, which is empowered to order the detention of individuals, when his fate is decided.

The rights to communicate with family members and to consult a legal practitioner are provided under the SOSMA. However, among the 146 individuals who were detained[89] under this Act from 2013 to November 2014, 11 detainees were neither informed of the reasons for their arrest nor were they allowed to communicate with the next of kin and to consult a lawyer for the first 8 days of their detention.[90]

---

[85] FIDH (2016)

[86] Ibid.

[87] Prevention of Crime (Amendment and Extension) Act, 2014 (Malaysia) Sec. 9(5)—Neither the person who is the subject of the inquiry nor a witness at an inquiry shall be represented by an advocate and solicitor at the inquiry except when his own evidence is being taken and recorded by the Inquiry Officer.

[88] Prevention of Terrorism Act, 2015 (Malaysia) Sec. 10(6)—Neither the person who is the subject of the inquiry nor a witness at an inquiry shall be represented by an advocate and solicitor at the inquiry except when his own evidence is being taken and recorded by the inquiry officer.

[89] In 2013, 3 persons were detained for promoting terrorism in Syria, 2 persons for recruiting Al-Qaeda Members and 110 persons for Sulu Invasion 2013. In 2014, 31 persons were detained for involvement with Islamic State in Iraq and Syria. (as cited in Suaram (2014), p. 4).

[90] Ibid.

2.7 Changes Introduced to Article 150 of the Constitution

Article 150(1) of the Federal Constitution of Malaysia, as discussed above in Sect. 2.6.1, originally empowered the executive to proclaim a state of emergency if it was satisfied that "a grave emergency… [existed] whereby the security or economic life" of Malaysia was threatened "by war or external aggression or internal disturbance". However, the Amendment Act of 1963 introduced substantial changes to this provision. For this Act, among other things, deleted the words "war or external aggression or internal disturbance" as grounds for invoking a declaration of emergency. Thus Article 150(1), as amended in 1963, authorizes the executive to proclaim an emergency without the precondition of any grave threats posed to the life of the nation. Consequently, the executive is invested with the absolute discretion to decide whether any given situation warrants the invocation of a state of emergency. This practice of not circumscribing the power of the executive to invoke a state of emergency to certain well-defined circumstances marks a clear departure from the practices followed in other democracies. For instance, in India, Article 352(1) of the Constitution, as amended in 1978 by the Constitution (Forty-Fourth) Amendment Act, confines the power to proclaim an emergency on the grounds of war or external aggression or armed rebellion. In the same vein, the Constitution of South Africa, 1996 provides that an emergency can be declared, among other things, on the grounds of "war, invasion, general insurrection".[91]

Furthermore, the Constitution of Malaysia does not stipulate any mechanisms for ensuring the effective scrutiny and timely revocation of an emergency. In this context, reference can be made to the constitutional arrangements in South Africa and Poland. The South African Constitution subjects a proclamation of emergency to increasing supermajorities of the Parliament. It stipulates that any proposal to extend a proclamation of emergency for a period not exceeding 3 months, in the first instance, must be supported by a simple majority of the Parliament while any subsequent extension of the proclamation would require "a supporting vote of at least 60 per cent of the members of the Parliament".[92] The utility of the South African model lies in its endeavour to empower the Parliament to act as a check on the executive's attempt to use emergency powers for extraneous purposes. The Constitution of Poland, 1997, on the other hand, stipulates that a proclamation of emergency cannot continue beyond 150 days,[93] thereby preventing the executive from continuing a proclamation beyond its imperative necessity.

In the absence of any effective constitutional safeguards governing the proclamation and administration of an emergency, emergencies have been declared and continued in Malaysia without the precondition of grave threats posed to the security and safety of the nation. Since the amendment introduced in 1963 to Article 150(1) of the Constitution, emergencies have been invoked in Malaysia on four occasions:

---

[91] Constitution of South Africa, 1996 (South Africa) Sec. 37(1)(a).

[92] Ibid., Sec. 37(2)(b).

[93] Constitution of Poland, 1997 (Poland) Art. 230(1) & (2).

(a) in 1964 to confront the issues arising out of the nation's conflict with its neighbours;
(b) in 1966 to contain the "internal jostling for power in Sarawak";
(c) in 1969 to put down the communal riot between Malays and Chinese, which adversely affected racial harmony in the country; and
(d) in 1977 in Kelantan to adequately put down "violent political demonstrations".[94]

It is striking that each of these emergencies were continued until December 2011[95]- long after the cessation of the hostilities which gave rise to them. Thus, it is evident that changes introduced to Article 150(1) of the Constitution were preferred in an effort to institute a permanent state of emergency in Malaysia. This is one of the most conspicuous examples of the exercise of the power of emergency.

The foregoing discussion, therefore, reveals that since the Federal Constitution of Malaysia came into force, the scope of the power of preventive detention enumerated therein and the restrictions on such power have gone through a number of amendments. It is further evident from the above discussion that the safeguards afforded to the detainee by the Constitution are not adequate for preventing abuse of the powers concerning preventive detention, which in turn provides sufficient leeway for the government of the day to resort to the extraordinary powers concerning preventive detention for suppressing political opponents and human rights activists. Over the years, several laws have been enacted in pursuance of Article 149. But the exercise of the power of preventive detention, particularly under the ISA, has been subject to criticism. The provisions regarding preventive detention under the ISA, SOSMA, PCA and POTA and their exercise will be dealt with in an in-depth manner in Chap. 4 of this thesis. It is further evident that by virtue of the substantial changes introduced to Article 150, the power to invoke and to continue an emergency can be used without the existence of grave threats posed to the life of the nation.

References

Aldred G. and Wynn J. (2012), It might have happened to your: Britain's "Guantanamo Bay" imprisonment without trial in WW2.
Ashutosh, D. (2014). *Law of preventive detention*. New Delhi: Universal Law Publishing.
Bari M. E. (2011). *Substantive independence of the judiciary under the constitutions of Malaysia and Bangladesh: A comparative study*. LLM Dissertation, University of Malaya, Kuala Lumpur, Malaysia.
Bari, M. E. (2017a). *States of emergency and the law: The experience of Bangladesh*. New York: Routledge.
Bari, M. E. (2017b). Preventive detention Laws in Bangladesh and their increased use during emergencies: A proposal for reform. *Oxford University Commonwealth Law Journal, 17*(1), 45–46.
Bonner, D. (1985). *Emergency powers in peacetime*. London: Sweet & Maxwell.

---

[94] Bari (2017a), p. 27.

[95] Ibid.

FIDH. (2016). *Worldwide movement for human rights, Malaysia: Continued arbitrary detention and solitary confinement of Maria Chin Abdullah, Chairperson of Bersih 2.0*. Available at https://www.fidh.org/en/issues/human-rights-defenders/malaysia-continued-arbitrary-detention-and-solitary-confinement-of.

Final Report of Federation of Malaya Constitutional Commission (Reid Commission). (1957). Submitted on 21 February 1957.

Harding, A. J., & Hatchard, J. (1993). Introduction. In A. J. Harding & J. Hatchard (Eds.), *Preventive detention and security law: A comparative survey* (p. 5). Boston: Martinus Nijhoff Publishers.

Human Rights Watch. (2004). *In the name of security counterterrorism and human rights abuses under Malaysia's Internal Security Act*. Available at https://www.hrw.org/reports/2004/malaysia0504/malaysia0504.pdf.

Hynes, G. (2017). *Defence of the realm act*. Available on https://encyclopedia.1914-1918-online.net/article/defence_of_the_realm_act_dora.

International Commission of Jurists. (1983). *States of Emergency: Their impact on human rights* 180, 394.

Iyer, V. (2000). *States of emergency: The Indian experience*. New Delhi: Butterworths India.

Jayakumar, S. (1978). Emergency powers in Malaysia: Development of the law 1957-1977. *Malaysia Law Journal, 1*, 9–24.

Martinez, J. S. (2005–2006). Inherent executive power: A comparative perspective. Yale Law Journal 115: 2480, 2496.

Munim, F. K. M. A. (1975). Rights of the citizens under the constitution and law. Bangladesh Institute of Law and International Affairs, Dacca. In A. J. Harding & J. Hatchard (Eds.), *Preventive detention and security law: A comparative survey*. Boston: Martinus Nijhoff Publishers.

Pandey, G. (2019). *Article 370: What happened with Kashmir and why it matters*. Available at https://www.bbc.com/news/world-asia-india-49234708.

Ramakrishnan, P. (2003). *Scrap the ISA Advisory Board*. Available at http://aliran.com/archives/ms/2003/0115.html.

Rudolph, H. (1984). The judicial review of administrative detention orders in Israel. In Y. Dinstein (Ed.), *Israel yearbook on human rights* (p. 12). Boston: Martinus Nijhoff Publishers.

Saravanamuttu, J. (2008). *Operation Lalang revisited: A call for the repeal of ISA*. Available at http://aliran.com/aliran-monthly/2008/2008-8/operation-lalang-revisited-a-call-for-the-repeal-of-isa/.

Sekhri, A. (2020). *Not fair, just or reasonable*. Available at https://www.thehindu.com/opinion/op-ed/not-fair-just-or-reasonable/article30905962.ece.

Sheridan, L. A. (1961). *Malaya and Singapore*. The Borneo Territories: The Development of Their Laws and Constitutions. Steven & Sons, London.

Suara Rakyat Malaysia (Suaram). (2014). *Malaysia: Human rights report overview*. Available at http://www.suaram.net/wordpress/wp-content/uploads/2014/12/Suaram-Human-Rights-Overview_2014_9-Dec.pdf.

Yatim, R. (1995). *Freedom under executive power in Malaysia: A study of executive supremacy*. Kuala Lumpur: Endowment Publications.

Chapter 3
The Quest for a Standard Preventive Detention Framework

Abstract Since the power of preventive detention carries the inherent risk of abuse, an attempt will be made in this chapter to evaluate the safeguards which have the merit of obviating the possibility of such abuse. Accordingly, this chapter, in the first place, will examine the safeguards stipulated by various human rights treaties and international principles for reducing the impact of the exercise of the power of preventive detention on the human rights of individuals. Subsequently, this chapter will turn its focus to the safeguards stipulated by some of the modern constitutions for constraining the scope of the power of preventive detention. Finally, in light of such analyses, this chapter would endeavour to design a standard framework concerning preventive detention, which would strike an appropriate balance between the necessity to respond to the threats posed to the security of a nation and to simultaneously preserve the right of a detainee to freedom from arbitrary detention.

3.1 Introduction

The exercise of the extraordinary power of preventive detention, as is evident from the discussion in Chap. 2, is often not circumscribed to formally declared periods of emergency notwithstanding its adverse impact on the human rights of individuals, particularly the right to liberty. Furthermore, the safeguards afforded to individuals kept in preventive custody have often proved inadequate for obviating the possibility of arbitrary detention. Consequently, there has often been a tendency to use the power of preventive detention as a means for deterring "legitimate political dissent and to imprison people for the non-violent exercise of fundamental human rights such as the rights to freedom of expression and belief and to freedom of association".[1]

Having gained an insight into the pathologies of the power of preventive detention in Chap. 2, an attempt will be made in this chapter to evaluate the safeguards stipulated by various human rights instruments and international principles to prevent abuse of the power of preventive detention. Second, this chapter will shed light on the procedural safeguards concerning preventive detention contained in the Constitutions of some of the modern democracies, such as, Pakistan and South

---

[1] Cook (1992), p. 11.

© Springer Nature Singapore Pte Ltd. 2020
M. E. Bari, S. Naz, *The Use of Preventive Detention Laws in Malaysia: A Case for Reform*, https://doi.org/10.1007/978-981-15-5811-5_3

Africa, for obviating the possibility of arbitrary encroachment on the human rights of individuals. Finally, in light of the examination of domestic and international safeguards, this chapter will seek to design a standard preventive detention framework encompassing the guarantees for preventing the abuse of the powers concerning preventive detention and also safeguarding the humane treatment of individuals kept in preventive custody.

3.2 The Right to Liberty and Permissibility of the Use of Preventive Detention under Human Rights Treaties and Various International Principles

Human rights are generally regarded as the universal, inviolable and inalienable moral rights of all individuals by dint of their membership of the human family.[2] Since rights seek to uphold the most fundamental interests of individuals, such as the interest in not being arbitrarily deprived of life or the interest in not being "subjected to torture or to cruel, inhuman or degrading treatment of punishment"[3] or the interest in not being arbitrarily deprived of liberty, it is imperative to take appropriate measures for the promotion and protection of these interests. As it was declared at the World Conference on Human Rights in 1993 in Vienna:

> All human rights are universal, indivisible and interdependent and interrelated. The international community must treat human rights globally in a fair and equal manner, on the same footing, and with the same emphasis. While the significance of national and regional particularities and various historical, cultural and religious backgrounds must be borne in mind, it is the duty of States, regardless of their political, economic and cultural systems, to promote and protect all human rights and fundamental freedoms.[4]

The right to liberty, as pointed out above, is one of the fundamental interests of individuals that merit protection and, as such, the international and regional human rights treaties, such as the International Covenant on Civil and Political Rights (ICCPR), 1966,[5] the European Convention on Human Rights and Fundamental Freedoms (ECHR), 1950,[6] and the American Convention on Human Rights (ACHR),

---

[2] Bari (2017a), p. 64.

[3] International Covenant on Civil and Political Rights (ICCPR), opened for signature on 16 December 1966, 999 UNTS 171 (entered into force on 23 March 1976), Art 7.

[4] UN Office of the High Commissioner for Human Rights (OHCHR) (2005), p. 5.

[5] International Covenant on Civil and Political Rights (ICCPR), opened for signature on 16 December 1966, 999 UNTS 171 (entered into force on 23 March 1976), in Art 9(1), among other things stipulates, that "Everyone has the right to liberty and security of person".

[6] European Convention for the Protection of Human Rights and Fundamental Freedoms (ECHR), opened for signature 4 November 1950, 213 UNTS 222 (entered into force on 3 September 1953), in art 5(1) provides, inter alia, that "Everyone has the right to liberty and security of person".

1969,[7] affirm this right of individuals in almost identical terms. Consequently, it can be argued that the implication of the recognition of this right in the human rights instruments is that "liberty should be the rule to which detention must be the exception and all States are bound by international law to respect and ensure everybody's right to liberty irrespective of their treaty obligations".[8]

The deprivation of an individual's liberty, as discussed earlier in Sect. 2.3, for preventing mischief to the state is permissible under the international human rights norms. However, these norms stipulate that preventive detention should not be arbitrary.[9] Furthermore, the ICCPR and other international principles, such as the Paris Minimum Standards of Human Rights Norms in a State of Emergency and the Body of Principles for the Protection of All Persons under Any Form of Detention or Imprisonment (BOP), stipulate that in order for detention of individuals to be valid, it must be on such grounds and in accordance with such procedure as are established by law.[10] Consequently, the Human Rights Committee has interpreted the term "arbitrariness" to mean something which should not "be equated with "against the law" but must be interpreted more broadly to include elements of inappropriateness, injustice, lack of predictability and due process of law."[11] Moreover, according to the UN Working Group on Arbitrary Detention[12]:

> a case of deprivation of liberty ceases to be arbitrary if it is consistent with domestic legislation and with the relevant international standards ... and in other relevant international instruments accepted by the State concerned. It is only necessary for it to be inconsistent with one of those criteria ... for the deprivation of liberty to be deemed arbitrary.[13]

---

[7] American Convention on Human Rights (ACHR), opened for signature on 22 November 1969, 1144 UNTS 123 (entered into force on 18 July 1978), in art 7(1), among other things, states that "Every person has the right to personal liberty and security."

[8] United Nations (2003).

[9] ICCPR Art. 9(1)—Among other things, stipulates that - "No one shall be subjected to arbitrary ... detention"; ECHR in art 5 stipulates several grounds for preventing arbitrary preventive detention; ACHR in art 7(3) states that "No one shall be subject to arbitrary" detention; ACPHR in art 6, among other things, stipulates that "no one may be arbitrarily ... detained".

[10] ICCPR Art. 9—The Paris Minimum Standards of Human Rights Norms in a State of Emergency, art 5; The Body of Principles for the Protection of All Persons under Any Form of Detention or Imprisonment.

[11] *Hugo van Alphen v. The Netherlands*, Communication No. 305/1988, U.N. Doc. CCPR/C/39/D/305/1988 (1990).

[12] The Working Group on Arbitrary Detention was established by resolution 1991/42 of the former Commission on Human Rights. Its mandate was clarified and extended by Commission's resolution 1997/50. The mandate was extended for a further three-year period by resolution 24/7 of 26 September 2013. One of the functions of the Working Group on Arbitrary Detention is to investigate cases of deprivation of liberty imposed arbitrarily or otherwise inconsistently with the relevant international standards set forth in the Universal Declaration of Human Rights or in the relevant international legal instruments accepted by the States concerned. Retrieved from http://www.ohchr.org/EN/Issues/Detention/Pages/WGADIndex.aspx

[13] UN Working Group on Arbitrary Detention: Mission to Peru (1999), para 60. Londras (2011), p. 54.

Thus, in light of the above discussion, it is evident that individuals can be deprived of their liberties for preventing "a danger to state security or public security"[14] on legal grounds and procedures established by domestic laws which conform to international standards.

3.2.1 Safeguards as to Preventive Detention under the International Human Rights Norms

It is striking that the ICCPR, which is considered the "most important universal instrument" on human rights with 170 state parties,[15] other than stating that no one should be subjected to arbitrary detention, does not stipulate effective safeguards for obviating the possibility of misuse of the extraordinary power of preventive detention. While the United States (US) and France did propose during the drafting stage of the ICCPR that the "most fundamental guarantees against arbitrary detention and some minimum rights of due process" should be explicitly rendered non-derogable for ensuring their observance in all circumstances,[16] this proposal was defeated due to opposition from the United Kingdom (UK). The UK's objection stemmed from its belief that the exigencies of a grave emergency may necessitate the dispensation of the guarantees against arbitrary detention.[17]

It seems that the omission to incorporate effective guarantees concerning preventive detention in the ICCPR has, subsequently, persuaded the Human Rights Committee (HRC)—a body entrusted with the responsibility of ensuring compliance of states parties with the human rights standards contained in the ICCPR—to extend the safeguards stipulated by Article 9 of the ICCPR, which are available to those arrested or detained on a criminal charge, to those kept in preventive custody. As the HRC in its General Comment No. 8 on Article 9, observed:

> if so-called preventive detention is used, for reasons of public security, it must be controlled by these same provisions, i.e., it must not be arbitrary and must be based on grounds and procedures established by law (para 1), information of the reasons must be given (para 2) and court control of the detention must be available (para 4) as well as compensation in the case of a breach (para 5).[18]

The HRC reiterated the above stance in *David Alberto Cámpora Schweizer v. Uruguay,* when it observed that:

---

[14] Rudolph, H (1984), p. 152.

[15] Meron (1986), 83; United Nations Treaty Collection, Chapter IV: Human Rights. Available at https://treaties.un.org/Pages/ViewDetails.aspx?src=TREATY&mtdsg_no=IV-3&chapter=4&clang=_en

[16] Oraa (1995), p. 106; United Nations (1949) (French and US Proposal); Hartman (1985), pp. 115–118.

[17] United Nations (1949) (UK Proposal); Hartman (1985), pp. 115–118.

[18] U.N. Human Rights Committee (1982), para 4.

[a]lthough administrative detention may not be objectionable in circumstances where the person concerned constitutes a clear and serious threat to society which cannot be contained in any other manner … the guarantees enshrined in … article 9 fully apply in such instances.[19]

Thus, it is evident from the above observations of the HRC that the safeguards stipulated in Article 9 of the ICCPR will be available to detainees kept in preventive custody. An attempt will now be made to evaluate the safeguards available under various human rights instruments to individuals who are detained under preventive detention laws.

(a) **Confining the Exercise of the Power of Preventive Detention to Emergencies**
    Notwithstanding the adverse impact of the exercise of the power of preventive detention on the liberty of individuals, the human rights treaties, such as the ICCPR, ECHR and ACHR, do not stipulate that such power should only be exercised during a state of emergency. Furthermore, the HRC while extending the safeguards contained in Article 9 of the ICCPR to individuals kept in preventive custody through its General Comment No. 8, did not seize on the opportunity to circumscribe the exercise of the power of preventive detention to declared periods of emergency.
    In light of the above omission of the human rights treaties, the International Commission of Jurists in one of the most comprehensive studies on states of emergency conducted in 1981 recommended that the power of preventive detention should only be exercised during an emergency declared to safeguard the security and integrity of the state.[20] The Special Rapporteur on States of Emergency has also endorsed this recommendation.[21]

(b) **Communication of the Grounds of Detention**
    The reason behind the requirement of communicating the grounds of detention to the detainee without any undue delay is to enable him to make an effective representation against the detention order. The ICCPR does not specifically impose an obligation on detaining authorities to promptly furnish the grounds of detention to those detained under preventive detention laws. However, it does stipulate in Article 9(2) that "anyone who is arrested shall be informed …of the reasons for his arrest and shall be promptly informed of any charges against him." Following the HRC's interpretation, as discussed above, of Article 9(2), it would seem that this safeguard would be available to individuals kept in preventive custody. However, the effectiveness of this safeguard in relation to

---

[19] *David Alberto Campora Schweixzer v. Uruguay*, Communication No. 66/1980, U.N. Doc. CCPR/C/OP/2 at 90 (1990). Available at http://www1.umn.edu/humanrts/undocs/newscans/66-1980.html

[20] International Commission of Jurists (1983), p. 429.

[21] Fitzpatrick (1994), pp. 45–46, Special Rapporteur of the Sub-Commission on Prevention of Discrimination and Protection of Minorities on human rights and states of emergency (1989), para 26, 66.

preventive detention cases is questionable. For it does not stipulate a specific time period for communicating the grounds of detention to the detainee.

Similar to the ICCPR, the ACHR in Article 7 (4) states, "[a]nyone who is detained shall be informed of the reasons for his detention and shall be promptly notified of the charge or charges against him." In stark contrast to the ICCPR and ACHR, the ECHR in Article 5(1) enumerates the circumstances which can warrant the exercise of the power of preventive detention. For instance, Article 5(1)(c) of the ECHR states preventive detention of an individual is permissible "where it is reasonably considered necessary to prevent his committing an offence or fleeing after having done so". Since Article 5(1) specifically provides for preventive detention, it can be argued that the safeguard stipulated in Article 5(2) obligating the detaining authority to promptly communicate the grounds of arrest to the detainee, is also available to an individual detained under a preventive detention law.

It is, therefore, evident that international and regional human rights treaties have kept the timeframe for communicating the grounds of detention to a detainee unspecified, thereby depriving him of the opportunity to make an effective representation against the detention. However, the Paris Minimum Standards of Human Rights Norms in a State of Emergency—adopted in 1984 by the International Law Association—seeks to fill this vacuum by stipulating that the detaining authority should inform the grounds of preventive detention to the detainee within 7 days of his detention.[22]

It should be stressed here that in order to further facilitate an effective representation by an individual against his detention order, it is imperative that the grounds communicated to him are clear and precise.[23] For if the grounds supplied to the detainee are vague or indefinite, his right to make the representation would inevitably be frustrated. However, it is striking that neither international nor regional human right treaties impose an obligation on detaining authorities to furnish the grounds of detention to the detainee in clear terms.

(c) **Right to Communicate with Lawyer and Family Members**

When detaining authorities engage in the stratagem of not publishing the name of an individual kept in preventive custody or of denying him access to a lawyer or to his family members, the detainee is rendered non-existent in the eyes of the world.[24] Consequently, such detention, known as detention incommunicado, enables detaining authorities to torture the detainee with impunity as information regarding such torture is unlikely to be disclosed to the public.[25] Such torture "in extreme cases" can also lead "to the death of" the detainee.[26] Notwithstanding the adverse impact of detention incommunicado on the

---

[22] Paris Minimum Standards of Human Rights Norms in a State of Emergency, Art. 5(2)(a).

[23] *Abdul Latif Mirza v Government of Bangladesh*, (1979) 31 DLR (AD) 1, 10.

[24] See above n 2, p. 430.

[25] Bari (2017b), p. 56.

[26] Ibid., p. 53; See above n 2, p. 159.

fundamental human rights of individuals, such as the right to life and the right not to be subjected to torture, the international human rights norms developed in the 1950s and 1960s, such as the ECHR, ICCPR and ACHR, do not stipulate any guarantees against such detention. However, the international principles developed in the 1980s for guiding the action of state authorities, stipulate guarantees against such detention. For instance, the BOP in Principle 18(1) stipulates that: "A detained ... person shall be entitled to communicate and consult with his legal counsel". This guarantee is further strengthened by Principle 18(1) of the BOP, which provides that: "A detained ... person shall be allowed adequate time and facilities for consultations with his legal counsel." Principle 19 of the BOP also extends to a detainee the right to communicate with his family members. As it provides:

A detained or imprisoned person shall have the right to be visited by and to correspond with, in particular, members of his family and shall be given adequate opportunity to communicate with the outside world, subject to reasonable conditions and restrictions as specified by law or lawful regulations.[27]

A similar guarantee can also be found in the Paris Minimum Standards of Human Rights Norms in a State of Emergency. First, the Paris Standards in Article 5(2)(b) provides that "[a]ny law providing for preventive or administrative detention shall secure the... minimum rights of the detainee: The right to communicate with, and consult, a lawyer of his own choice, at any time after detention." Second, the Paris Standards in Article 5(2)(f) entitle the detainee to regular visits by family members. More importantly, since dispensation of these guarantees, as pointed out above, can lead to breach of fundamental human rights of detainees, the Standards have gone further by stipulating that these guarantees should be non-derogable, thereby providing them stronger protection.

It is evident from the above discussion that the international standards do not provide a specific timeframe within which a detainee should be given access to his lawyer and family members. However, in this context, the Siracusa Principles on the Limitation and Derogation Provisions in the International Covenant on Civil and Political Rights, 1984 provides useful guidance. For it recommends that detention incommunicado should not continue for more than 3–7 days.[28]

(d) **Right to Have the Lawfulness of the Detention Order Reviewed**

The utility of a writ of *habeas corpus* in preventing arbitrary encroachment on the liberty of individuals was recognized by the Working Group on Arbitrary Detention in its 2010 Report: "*Habeas Corpus* is a legal procedure which is an undeniable right of all individuals and one of the most effective remedies against challenging arbitrary detention".[29] The Working Group in further emphasizing this utility submitted that

---

[27] The Body of Principles for the Protection of All Persons under Any Form of Detention or Imprisonment, Principle 19.

[28] UN Commission on Human Rights (1984), p. 54.

[29] United Nations Human Rights Council (2010), p. 76.

habeas corpus... should not be regarded as a mere element in the right to a fair trial but in a country governed by the rule of law, as a personal right which cannot be derogated from even in a state of emergency.[30]

Accordingly, the major human treaties, namely, the ECHR,[31] ICCPR,[32] and ACHR,[33] stipulate that all detainees, regardless of whether they are being held in connection with criminal offences or are being kept in preventive custody, have the right to initiate legal proceedings to challenge the lawfulness of the detention before a judicial authority, which in turn should decide the matter expeditiously and subsequently order the release of the detainee if the detention is found to be unlawful.[34] Furthermore, the Human Rights Committee in its General Comment No. 8 stated that the exercise of the power of preventive detention is not readily justifiable by making reference to grave threats, such as conflict, war or state of exception, to the security of the nation and as such the right, among other things, to challenge the lawfulness of the detention should be made available to an individual kept in preventive custody.[35]

(e) **Right to Compensation for Unlawful Detention**

Among the human rights treaties, only the ECHR and ICCPR contain provisions concerning the right of a detainee to be compensated financially if his detention was unlawful. Article 5(5) of the ECHR provides that: "everyone who has been the victim of ... detention in contravention of the provisions of ... [Article 5][36] shall have an enforceable right to compensation." In the same vein, Article 9(5) of the ICCPR stipulates that: "Anyone who has been the victim of unlawful ... detention shall have an enforceable right to compensation."

It can be argued that imposing an obligation to provide monetary compensation to those who have been unlawfully deprived of their liberty would deter the executive branch of government from arbitrarily detaining an enormous number of individuals. For it will be aware that such "arbitrary stockpiling" will come at a steep price.[37]

It is evident from the above discussion that the human rights treaties do not:

(a) confine the exercise of the power of preventive detention to states of emergency;
(b) specify a time limit for communicating the grounds of detention to an individual kept in preventive custody; and
(c) bar detention incommunicado.

---

[30] Ibid., para 78.

[31] European Convention for the Protection of Human Rights and Fundamental Freedoms, 1950, 213 U.N.T.S. 221, Nov. 4, 1950, Art. 7(6).

[32] International Covenant on Civil and Political Rights, Dec. 19, 1966, 999 U.N.T.S. 171, Art. 9(4).

[33] American Convention on Human Rights, Nov. 21, 1969, 1144 U.N.T.S. 143, Art. 5(4).

[34] See above n 1, 25.

[35] United Nation (2009), p. 104.

[36] Article 5 of the ECHR is concerning the right to liberty and security.

[37] Ackerman (2006), p. 54.

Furthermore, the human rights treaties, strikingly, do not prescribe a maximum period of preventive detention. It is pertinent to note here that the absence of such a guarantee often persuades state authorities to subject individuals to indefinite or prolonged detention, which in turn can lead to the violation of fundamental human rights. In this context, the observations of the United Nations (UN) Special Rapporteur on torture at the "Expert Meeting on the situation of detainees held at the US Naval Base at Guantanamo Bay" with respect to the adverse consequences of indefinite detention is noteworthy: "the greater the uncertainty regarding the length of time, the greater the risk of serious mental pain and suffering to the inmate that may constitute cruel, inhuman or degrading treatment or punishment or even torture".[38] There is empirical evidence to support this assertion of the Special Rapporteur. For instance, a 2014 US Senate Report on the techniques used for interrogating individuals, who had been detained in Guantanamo Bay for indefinite periods, found that detainees were commonly exposed to inhuman torture methods, such as waterboarding, sleep deprivation for up to "180 hours" at a time, "rectal hydration or rectal feeding" and "ice water baths".[39] The indefinite detention coupled with the torture in Guantanamo caused the death of a detainee and led several detainees to exhibit "psychological and behavioral issues, including hallucinations, paranoia and attempts at self-harm and self-mutilation".[40]

Therefore, in light of the foregoing discussion, it can be concluded that the safeguards stipulated by the human rights treaties are not adequate for obligating states parties to ensure the maintenance of a delicate balance between protecting national security and at the same time safeguarding the essential human rights of individuals. Although the international standards developed in the 1980s seek to plug some of these loopholes in the human rights treaties, these standards do not bind states in the same manner as treaties.

Having critically examined the safeguards concerning preventive detention contained in various international instruments, an attempt will now be made to discuss the safeguards provided to detainees by some of the modern constitutions.

3.3   The Guarantees Concerning Preventive Detention Contained in the 1973 Constitution of Pakistan and the 1996 Constitution of South Africa

It is a common feature of the constitutions of modern democracies to permit the exercise of the power of preventive detention during both emergency and non-emergency situations. However, some of these constitutions stipulate effective safeguards for preventing the abuse of the power of preventive detention. In this context,

---

[38] United Nations High Commissioner for Human Rights (2013).

[39] United States Senate Select Committee on Intelligence (2012), pp. 3–4; See above n 2, 158–159.

[40] United States Senate Select Committee on Intelligence (2012), pp. 4; See above n 25, pp. 52–53.

the safeguards prescribed by the Constitution of Pakistan, 1973 and the Constitution of South Africa, 1996 deserve special attention.

3.3.1 The 1973 Constitution of Pakistan and the Provisions Concerning Preventive Detention

Pakistan emerged as an independent Dominion on 14 August 1947 after the British Parliament passed the Indian Independence Act partitioning the Subcontinent.[41] Since emerging as an independent nation, Pakistan has enacted three permanents Constitutions in 1956, 1962 and 1973 respectively.[42] Following in the footsteps of the colonial legislative framework and the Constitution of India, 1950, the provisions concerning preventive detention found a prominent place in all these Pakistani Constitutions. Thus, both Pakistan and Malaysia not only share a colonial legal heritage, but their preventive detention framework are also heavily drawn from the Indian Constitution.

It is pertinent to note here that the 1973 Constitution of Pakistan, which is still in force, came into force on 14 August 1973—less than 2 years after the Eastern Province of Pakistan had emerged as an independent nation under the name of Bangladesh following a bloody war of independence. Furthermore, prior to the enactment of 1973 Constitution, the power of preventive detention had often been used to persecute the inhabitants of East Pakistan (now Bangladesh).[43] Accordingly, in order to obviate the possibility of abuse of the power of preventive detention, the framers endeavoured to incorporate effective safeguards in the 1973 Constitution for mitigating the harshness of the exercise of such power.

The Constitution of Pakistan, 1973 in Article 10(4) empowers the Parliament to make laws permitting the executive to preventively detain "persons acting in a manner prejudicial to the integrity, security or defence of Pakistan or any part thereof or external affairs of Pakistan or public order or the maintenance of supplies or services." Thus, it is evident that in the same manner as the Constitution of India, as discussed in Sect. 2.4, the 1973 Constitution of Pakistan enables the executive to exercise the power of preventive detention on vague grounds.

However, unlike the Indian Constitution, the Constitution of Pakistan, as will be evident from the forthcoming discussion, provides effective safeguards to individuals kept in preventive custody. An attempt will now be made to examine these safeguards.

(a) **Review of a Preventive Detention Order by an Advisory Board**
     Article 10(4) of the Constitution of Pakistan originally provided that an individual could not be kept in preventive custody for more than a month without

---

[41] Bari (2017a), p. 39.

[42] Ibid, pp. 39–40.

[43] Ibid, pp. 117–118.

the concurrence of an Advisory Board. Thus, the Constitution did not originally authorise the executive to deprive the liberty of an individual without any trial or review for more than a month. However, the Constitution (Third Amendment) Act, 1975 sought to undermine the safeguard originally stipulated by Article 10(4) of the Constitution. For the Third Amendment extended the time period for which a person can be preventively detained without the concurrence of an Advisory Board from 1 month to 3 months.[44] Notwithstanding the extension of the time period for which an individual can be detained without reference to an Advisory Board, Justice MR Kayani in *Khan Ghulam Mohammed Khan Loondkhawar v. The State*[45] shed light on the importance of the safeguard contained in Article 10(4) in the following terms:

It is as though the Constitution were saying to the detaining authority: "I appreciate the occasional urgency of a situation when you may be called upon to take away the liberty of a citizen on your own responsibility for law and order, but my experience of your past, what with your implicit trust in police reports and what with your doubtful morals in the political field, constrains me to rely on your discretion for no more than 3 months."[46]

Furthermore, in order to deprive the executive of the opportunity to influence the functioning of the Advisory Board by packing it with loyalists, the Constitution authorizes the Chief Justice of Pakistan to constitute the Advisory Board.[47] The 1973 Constitution also confines the membership of the Advisory Board to individuals who are or have been judges of the Supreme Court of Pakistan or a High Court.[48] Thus, unlike the Constitution of India, which empowers the executive to constitute the Advisory Board,[49] the Constitution of Pakistan ensures the independence of the Advisory Board from the whims of the executive branch of government when determining the necessity to continue the detention of an individual.

In order to enable the Advisory Board to carry out its functions in a satisfactory manner, the 1973 Constitution imposes a further obligation on the detaining authority to "furnish" to the Board "all documents relevant to the case".[50]

(b) **Communication of the Grounds of Detention within a Specified Time Period**

In order to enable an individual kept in preventive custody to make an effective representation against his detention order, the Constitution of Pakistan, 1973 under Article 10(5) originally imposed an obligation on the detaining authorities to inform the detainee of the grounds of detention "as soon as may be, but not later than one week" from the day he was detained.[51] Thus, 11 years

---

[44] Constitution of Pakistan, 1973 (Pakistan) Art. 10(4).

[45] *Khan Ghulam Mohammed Khan Loondkhawar v. The State* [1957] PLD Lah. 497.

[46] Ibid., p. 504.

[47] Constitution of Pakistan, 1973 (Pakistan) Art. 10(4).

[48] Constitution of Pakistan, 1973 (Pakistan) Art. 10(4).

[49] Constitution of India, 1950 (India) Art. 22(4)(a).

[50] Constitution of Pakistan, 1973 (Pakistan) Art. 10(6).

[51] Constitution of Pakistan, 1973 (Pakistan) Art. 10(5).

before the adoption of the Paris Standards, as discussed earlier in 3.2.1(b), the Constitution of Pakistan specified a time period of 7 days within which the grounds of detention had to be supplied to the detainee. However, the Constitution (Third Amendment) Act, which was passed in February 1975 by an emergency regime, adversely affected this safeguard by increasing the time period within which the grounds of detention were to be communicated to a detainee from 7 to 15 days.[52] Notwithstanding such an increase, the provision contained in Article 10(5) is still an improvement on the safeguards contained in the Constitution of India, 1950, which keeps the timeframe for communicating the grounds of detention to the detainee indeterminate.[53] Furthermore, human rights treaties, which, as discussed earlier in 3.2.1(b), do not fix the time period for informing the grounds of detention to the detainee.

(c) **Authority to Determine the Place of Detention and to Fix a Subsistence Allowance**

The Constitution of Pakistan, 1973 also empowers the Advisory Board to determine the place of detention of a preventively detained individual and to fix a reasonable subsistence allowance for the family of the detainee.[54] Thus, the Constitution not only obviates the possibility of secret detention but also authorizes Board to extend some form of monetary assistance to the family members of a detainee so as to ensure their survival during the continuation of the detention.

(d) **Stipulation of the Maximum Period of Detention**

Unlike the Constitution of India, 1950, which does not specify a maximum time-limit for keeping an individual in preventive custody, the Constitution of Pakistan stipulates that an individual can be preventively detained for no longer than 8 months "for acting in a manner prejudicial to public order", and 12 months in any other case.[55] Thus the Constitution of Pakistan by stipulating the maximum period of preventive detention obviates the possibility of indefinite or prolonged detention.

It is, therefore, evident from the above discussion that the Constitution of Pakistan enumerates certain effective safeguards for preventing the possibility of arbitrary encroachment on the rights of an individual.

---

[52] Constitution of Pakistan, 1973 (Pakistan) Art. 10(5).

[53] Constitution of India, 1950 (India) Art. 22(5).

[54] Constitution of Pakistan, 1973 Art. 10(8).

[55] Constitution of Pakistan, 1973 Art. 10(7).

3.3.2   The Constitution of South Africa, 1996

From 1948 to 1991, the government of the National Party implemented a policy of racial segregation in South Africa,[56] which became known as apartheid.[57] During the apartheid era, the regime used proclamations of emergency and the power of preventive detention as the most convenient means to violently persecute those who opposed its racist policies.[58] Referring to the adverse impact on the human rights of individuals during the apartheid era, Justice Ackerman observed: "No right-minded person in any society which claimed to be democratic and based on freedom and equality would today even try to justify these limitations."[59] In light of the erosion of human rights of individuals during the apartheid era due to, among other things, the arbitrary exercise of the powers of emergency and preventive detention, the Constitution of South Africa, which was promulgated on 18 December 1996, enumerates effective guarantees for obviating the possibility of using the extraordinary powers of emergency and preventive detention as vehicles for imposing unwarranted restrictions on the fundamental human rights of individuals. Taking into account the extensive guarantees of human rights coupled with effective safeguards for ensuring the enjoyment of the core rights at all times, commentators have widely hailed the Constitution of South Africa as one of the most progressive constitutions in the world.[60] Accordingly, an attempt will now be made to evaluate the safeguards, including those for mitigating the harshness of the exercise of the power of preventive detention, contained in the Constitution of South Africa.

3.3.2.1   The Safeguards Concerning Emergency Powers and Preventive Detention Enumerated in the Constitution of South Africa for Reducing Impact on the Human Rights of Individuals

It should be stressed here that the apartheid era was based on a system of parliamentary supremacy, which essentially meant that the Parliament could make or unmake any law regardless of its detrimental impact on the human rights of individuals. As the Appellate Division—then the highest court of law in South Africa—observed in *Sachs v Minister of Justice*[61]: "Parliament … [could] make any encroachment it please[d] upon the life, liberty and property of any individual subject to its sway."[62]

---

[56] Dyzenhaus (2010), p. XI.

[57] Apartheid, an Afrikaans word meaning "apartness," describes an ideology of racial segregation that served as the basis for white domination of the South African State from 1948 to 1991.

[58] See above n 2, pp. 133–134, 137.

[59] *Ferreira v. Levin NO and Others*; *Vryenhoek v Powell NO and Others*, 1996(1) SA 984 (CC), 1996(1) BCLR 1 (CC) at 1015 (para 51).

[60] Heap and Morgans (2007), p. 134.

[61] *Sachs v Minister of Justice* (1934) AD 11 (A).

[62] Ibid., p. 37.

Accordingly, Section 2, which is contained in Chap. 1—titled "the Founding Provisions"—of the Constitution of the Republic of South Africa,[63] does away with the notion of parliamentary supremacy by affirming the supremacy of the Constitution, thus: "This Constitution is the supreme law of the Republic; law or conduct inconsistent with it is invalid, and the obligations imposed by it must be fulfilled."

The South African Bill of Rights is entrenched in Chapter 2 of the 1996 Constitution of South Africa and is affirmed by the Constitution itself as "a corner-stone of democracy in South Africa".[64] One of the many fundamental rights guaranteed by the Bill of Rights is the right to freedom and security of individuals, which finds expression in Section 12(1) of the Chapter 2 of the Constitution in the following terms:

Everyone has the right to freedom and security of the person which includes the right

(a) not to be deprived of freedom arbitrarily or without just cause;
(b) not to be detained without trial;
(c) to be free from all forms of violence from either public or private sources;
(d) not to be tortured in any way; and
(e) not to be treated or punished in a cruel, inhuman or degrading way.

It is pertinent to stress here that although the Constitution of South Africa authorizes the declaration of a state of emergency and the exercise of the power of preventive detention, it incorporates a number of safeguards for reducing the impact on the human rights of individuals. First, the Constitution explicitly incorporates the principles of proportionality and non-derogation. The Constitution recognizes the principle of proportionality, which is premised on the idea that "there should be a reasonable relationship or balance between an end and the means used to achieve that end",[65] by stipulating in Section 37(4) that any legislation "may derogate from the Bill of Rights only to the extent that … the derogation is strictly required by" the exigencies of an emergency. Thus, any legislation passed during an emergency limiting human rights has to be a proportionate response for dealing with the exigencies of the crisis, "both as a matter of degree and duration".[66] On the other hand, the principle of non-derogation, which is based on the notion that some human rights are "too fundamental and too precious" and consequently, should not be suspended even during a state of emergency,[67] has found expression in a tabular form in Section 37(5) of the Constitution of South Africa. The rights which have been recognized as non-derogable in the Constitution include the right to life, the right not to be subjected to torture, cruel, inhuman and degrading treatment and the right to freedom from slavery.

Second, the Constitution stipulates further safeguards for supplementing the principles of non-derogation and proportionality. For instance, the Constitution

---

[63] The Constitution of Republic of South Africa, 1996 (South Africa).
[64] The Constitution of Republic of South Africa, 1996 (South Africa) Chapter 2, Art 7.
[65] Kirk (1997), p. 2.
[66] Hartman (1981), p. 17.
[67] Iyer (1999), pp. 134–135.

limits the power to declare a state of emergency to certain well-defined circumstances, such as "war, invasion, general insurrection, disorder, natural disaster".[68] Furthermore, it stipulates that in order for a proclamation of emergency and the consequent derogating measures to remain in force, they must be periodically approved by increasing supermajorities of the Parliament—any attempt to extend a state of emergency for a period of three months will require the support of a simple majority of the Parliament and thereafter any subsequent extension of the emergency will require the support of at least 60 per cent of the members of the Parliament.[69] The incorporation of these safeguards in the Constitution obviates the possibility of a state of emergency being used to arbitrarily deprive individuals of the enjoyment of their fundamental rights.

Third, since the extraordinary scope of the power of preventive detention often persuades the executive to use it, as pointed out earlier in Sect. 2.4, during emergency situations for arbitrarily depriving individuals, including political adversaries, of their liberty, the Constitution also provides detailed guarantees in Sections 37(6) and 37(7) for obviating the possibility of such abuse, in the following terms:

(6) Whenever anyone is detained without trial in consequence of a derogation of rights resulting from a declaration of a state of emergency, the following conditions must be observed:

   (a) An adult family member or friend of the detainee must be contacted as soon as reasonably possible, and informed that the person has been detained.
   (b) A notice must be published in the national Government Gazette within 5 days of the person being detained, stating the detainee's name and place of detention and referring to the emergency measure in terms of which that person has been detained.
   (c) The detainee must be allowed to choose, and be visited at any reasonable time by, a medical practitioner.
   (d) The detainee must be allowed to choose, and be visited at any reasonable time by, a legal representative.
   (e) A court must review the detention as soon as reasonably possible, but no later than 10 days after the date the person was detained, and the court must release the detainee unless it is necessary to continue the detention to restore peace and order.
   (f) A detainee who is not released in terms of a review under paragraph (e), or who is not released in terms of a review under this paragraph, may apply to a court for a further review of the detention at any time after 10 days have passed since the previous review, and the court must release the detainee unless it is still necessary to continue the detention to restore peace and order.
   (g) The detainee must be allowed to appear in person before any court considering the detention, to be represented by a legal practitioner at those hearings, and to make representations against continued detention.
   (h) The state must present written reasons to the court to justify the continued detention of the detainee, and must give a copy of those reasons to the detainee at least 2 days before the court reviews the detention.

(7) If a court releases a detainee, that person may not be detained again on the same grounds unless the state first shows a court good cause for re-detaining that person.

Thus, it is evident from a perusal of the above provisions that the Constitution of South Africa, among other things, bars detention incommunicado by requiring

---

[68] The Constitution of Republic of South Africa, 1996 (South Africa) Chapter 2, Section 37(1).
[69] The Constitution of Republic of South Africa, 1996 (South Africa) Chapter 2, Section 37(2)(b).

detaining authorities to issue a Gazette notifying the details pertaining to an individual's detention and allowing the detainee access to the outside world, thereby limiting the possibility of torture and mistreatment of individuals kept in preventive custody. Furthermore, it explicitly allows a detainee to have his detention order reviewed before a court of law within 10 days of his detention and in order to ensure the effectiveness of such a review, it obligates the detaining authority to communicate to him the grounds of detention at least 2 days before the review. If the previous review is unsuccessful, then the detainee can apply for a further review 10 days after the unsuccessful attempt.

Additionally, the Constitution makes some of the safeguards concerning preventive detention non-derogable during the continuation of an emergency. These non-derogable safeguards, among other things, include the following:

(a) the right to be informed of the grounds of detention "with sufficient detail to answer",[70]
(b) the right to challenge the legality of the detention before a court of law and, "if the detention is unlawful, to be released",[71] and
(c) the right to be represented by a lawyer.[72]

It is evident from the above discussion that through the enumeration of effective guarantees in the Constitution, it is possible to maintain a certain degree of respect for the human rights of individuals, including the right to protection from arbitrary deprivation of liberty and the right to freedom from torture, while responding to grave threats posed to the life of the nation.

3.4   Developing a Standard Preventive Detention Framework

Having gained a detailed insight into the safeguards that are essential for maintaining an appropriate balance between the necessity to exercise the power of preventive detention for responding to threats posed to the security of the nation and to simultaneously uphold the human rights of individuals, an attempt will now be made to develop a standard preventive detention framework. Such a framework should be incorporated in the constitution of a nation. For a constitutional framework stipulating effective guarantees concerning preventive detention will act as a check on the executive's tendency to arbitrarily detain an enormous number of individuals. The standard framework entrenched in domestic constitutions should not only contain the following safeguards but should simultaneously make them non-derogable under all circumstances.

---

[70] The Constitution of Republic of South Africa, 1996 (South Africa) Chapter 2, Section 35(3)(a).

[71] The Constitution of Republic of South Africa, 1996 (South Africa) Chapter 2, Section 35(2)(d).

[72] The Constitution of Republic of South Africa, 1996 (South Africa) Chapter 2, Section 35(3)(f).

(a) **Confining the Use of Preventive Detention to Declared Periods of Emergency**

Taking into account the adverse impact of the power of preventive detention on the human rights individuals, the ICJ has consistently recommended the necessity to confine the exercise of such power to a state of emergency. It proposed such a limitation on the exercise of the power of preventive detention, as pointed out earlier in 3.2.1(a), for the first time in 1981. Thus in the ICJ's estimation when the danger posed to the security and safety of the nation ceases to exist, the executive's power to use preventive detention "should come to an end".[73] Eight years later in 1989, the ICJ reiterated before the United Nations Sub-Commission on Prevention and Protection of Minorities that preventive detention can "only be adopted during an officially declared state of emergency which threatens the life of the nation".[74] Most recently in February 2012, the ICJ in its submission to the Working Group on Arbitrary Detention not only echoed its previous recommendation of confining the exercise of the power of preventive detention to declared periods of emergency but also sought to impose further restrictions on the power. For it stated that the power should only be used "to the extent strictly necessary to meet a threat to the life of a nation".[75] It then follows that the power of preventive detention "should not be resorted to" even during a state of emergency "if more effective and less severe means of defence against the danger are available".[76]

It can be argued that limiting the power of preventive detention to states of emergency would diminish the possibility of resort to such an extraordinary measure for arbitrarily depriving individuals of their liberty in times of peace.

(b) **Right to be Informed of the Grounds of Detention within the Shortest Possible Timeframe**

In light of the specific recommendation, as discussed earlier in 3.2.1(b), of the Paris Standards, the detaining authority should communicate the grounds of detention to the detainee within 7 days of his detention for enabling him to make an effective representation against the order of detention.[77] It should be further obligatory on the detaining authority to ensure that the grounds communicated to the detainee are sufficient in detail and are articulated in clear language. For doing so would enable the detainee to gain a clear insight into the grounds which formed the basis of the detaining authority's belief that he might commit acts prejudicial to the security and safety of the state and would, consequently, further bolster his chances of making an effective representation

---

[73] See above n 2, p. 159.

[74] Special Rapporteur of the Sub-Commission on Prevention of Discrimination and Protection of Minorities on human rights and states of emergency (1989), para. 66.

[75] International Commission of Jurists (2012), http://icj.wpengine.netdna-cdn.com/wp-content/uploads/2012/06/Submission-working-Group-detention-analysis-brief-2012.pdf.

[76] See above n 14, p. 152.

[77] Paris Minimum Standards of Human Rights Norms in a State of Emergency, Art. 5(2)(a); Harding and Hatchard (1993), p. 8.

against the detention.[78] In this context, Justice Kemaluddin Hossain in *Abdul Latif Mirza v Government of Bangladesh*[79] observed:

> Grounds [to be communicated to the detainee] … must be clear, precise and give such information to the detenu[80] that he could make … [an effective] representation; it must not be vague or indefinite and that the grounds must be relatable to the existing facts.[81]

(c) **Right of the Detainee to Make a Representation against an Order of Detention before an Independent Body**

An individual kept in preventive custody should be given the opportunity to make a representation against his order of detention before an Advisory Body within 10–30 days of his detention.[82] In order for the Advisory Board to be independent of the wishes of the executive branch of government while considering the representation of the detainee, it should be constituted by the Chief Justice of the nation and should be solely composed of individuals who are or have been judges of the superior courts.[83] Furthermore, the Advisory Board should be authorized, after considering the representation of the detainee, to recommend the release of the detainee if his detention is no longer considered necessary for dealing with the dangers posed to the safety and security of the nation. The government in turn should be obliged to release the detainee in pursuance of the recommendation of the Board.[84]

(d) **Right to Protection from Detention Incommunicado**

In light of the inextricable link, as pointed out earlier in 3.2.1(a), between detention incommunicado and torture, it is contended that an individual kept in preventive custody should be given access to the outside world, particularly to family members and a lawyer, without any inordinate delay. As to the specific timeframe within which such access should be granted, the Siracusa Principles, as pointed out earlier in 3.2.1(c), propose such a timeframe to be no more than 3–7 days.

(e) **Right to Challenge the Legality of the Order of Detention**

A detainee should be given the right to challenge the legality of his detention order in pursuance of a writ of *habeas corpus* within 10–30 days of his detention.[85] Subsequently, the judiciary should "scrutinize the allegations of fact as well as grounds for the detention" in order to determine whether there is any

---

[78] *Rowshen Bijaya Shaukat Ali Khan v Government of East Pakistan*, [1965] 17 PLD 241, 247 and 256.

[79] *Abdul Latif Mirza v Government of Bangladesh* [1979] 31 DLR (AD) 1.

[80] In the 1970s and 1980s, the judges in Bangladesh popularly used the word 'detenu' instead of detainee.

[81] *Abdul Latif Mirza v Government of Bangladesh*, [1979] 31 DLR (AD) 1, 10.

[82] This timeframe is recommended on the basis of section 37(6)(2) of the Constitution of South Africa, 1996 and article 5(2)(d) of the Paris Minimum Standards.

[83] Constitution of Pakistan, 1973 (Pakistan) Art. 10(4).

[84] Harding and Hatchard (1993), p. 9; Oraa (1995), p. 113.

[85] Constitution of South Africa, Chapter 2, Section 37(6)(e); Paris Minimum Standards, art 5.

basis for continuing the detention due to the executive's suspicion that the detainee might commit activities endangering state security.[86] To this end, Justice Hamoodur Rahman in *Mir Abdul Baqi Baluch v Government of Pakistan*[87] observed:

> What the court is concerned with is to see that the executive or administrative authority had before it sufficient materials upon which a reasonable person could have come to the conclusion that the requirements of law were satisfied. It is not uncommon that even high executive authorities act upon the basis of information supplied to them by their subordinates. In the circumstances, it cannot be said that it would be unreasonable for the Court, in the proper exercise of its constitutional duty, to insist upon a disclosure of the materials upon which the authority acted so that it should satisfy itself that the authority had not acted in an 'unlawful manner'.[88]

(f) **Fixing a Maximum Time-limit for Keeping a Detainee in Preventive Custody**

It is pertinent to note here that during a state of emergency, ample means and resources are made available to the executive branch of government for containing the threats posed to the life of the nation. Consequently, the ICJ, in its comprehensive Study on States of Emergency conducted in 1983, concluded that it is highly unlikely that any crisis threatening the security and integrity of the nation can continue beyond 6 months.[89] Accordingly, it is necessary for a constitution to stipulate a maximum time-limit of 6 months on the continuation of a state of emergency. The stipulation of a such a time-limit obviates the possibility of undue lingering of a state of emergency for extraneous purposes. It should be stressed here that in an effort to prevent the continuation of an emergency beyond its imperative necessities, it is not uncommon for modern constitutions to fix the maximum period of emergency. In this context, reference can be made to the Constitution of Poland, 1997, which stipulates that a proclamation of emergency cannot continue for more than 5 months.[90] Thus, the Constitution of Poland specifies a more rigorous safeguard for ensuring the timely termination of an emergency.

In light of the necessity to set a time-limit of 6 months on the continuation of a state of emergency, it can also be argued that the executive should not be empowered to keep an individual in preventive custody for more than 6 months. The enumeration of such a time-limit obviates the possibility of indefinite detention of individuals and as such, contributes towards maintaining respect for the fundamental human rights of individuals. For indefinite detention, as has been discussed earlier in 3.2.1, can lead to violation of the right to life and the right to freedom from torture.

---

[86] Harding and Hatchard (1993).

[87] *Mir Abdul Baqi Baluch v Government of Pakistan* [1968] PLD (SC) 313.

[88] Quoted in *Aruna Sen v Government of the People's Republic of Bangladesh & Others*, [1974] 3 CLC (HCD) 1, 15.

[89] See above n 20, P. 459.

[90] The Constitution of the Republic of Poland, 1997 (Poland) Art 230(1) and (2).

(g) **Right of the Detainee to Claim Financial Compensation**

Finally, in the event an individual is preventively detained due to his political belief or without any viable reason, he should not only be entitled to an immediate release but also to monetary compensation from the government for being subjected to such arbitrary detention.[91] The stipulation of a provision, as pointed earlier in 3.2.1(e), providing for monetary compensation would act as an effective safeguard against the executive tendency to use the power of preventive detention for detaining an enormous number of individuals. In this context, the observations of Bruce Ackerman are noteworthy:

> The emergency administration should be obliged to pay these costs out of its own budget, and this prospect will concentrate the bureaucratic mind on what is most vital in a democracy. The arbitrary stockpiling of suspects in prison will come with a price, and one that all of us will pay in taxes. The security forces will have new incentives to spend time and energy determining who has been snared by mistake.[92]

It should be stressed here the stipulation of the above safeguards concerning preventive detention in the constitution of a nation would go a long way to strike an appropriate balance between the necessity to respond to the threats posed to the security of a nation and to simultaneously preserve the right of a detainee to freedom from arbitrary detention. Accordingly, an attempt will be made in the next chapter, i.e. Chap. 4, to use the standard preventive detention framework designed above as a yardstick to expose the weaknesses of the Malaysian Constitution's provisions concerning preventive detention and preventive detention laws, namely the ISA, SOSMA, PCA and POTA. An attempt will also made to shed light on the exercise of the power of preventive detention under these laws.

References

Ackerman, B. (2006). *Before the next attack: Preserving civil liberties in an age of terrorism.* New Haven: Yale University Press.

Annual report. of the Special Rapporteur of the Sub-Commission on Prevention of Discrimination and Protection of Minorities on human rights and states of emergency, UN Doc E/CN.4/Sub.2/1989/SR.32. Available at https://digitallibrary.un.org/record/253914?ln=en.

Bari, M. E. (2017a). *States of emergency and the law: The experience of Bangladesh.* New York: Routledge.

Bari, M. E. (2017b). Preventive detention Laws in Bangladesh and their increased use during emergencies: A proposal for reform. *Oxford University Commonwealth Law Journal, 17*(1), 45–46.

Cook, H. (1992). Preventive detention—international standards and the protection of the individual. In S. Frankowski & D. Shelton (Eds.), *Preventive detention: A comparative and international law perspectives* (p. 11). Dordrecht: Springer.

---

[91] International Covenant on Civil and Political Rights (ICCPR), opened for signature on 16 December 1966, 999 UNTS 171 (entered into force on 23 March 1976), Art. 9(5).

[92] See above n 37, p. 54.

De Londras, F. (2011). *Detention in the 'war on terror': Can human rights fight Back?* Cambridge: Cambridge University Press.

Dyzenhaus, D. (2010). *Hard cases in wicked legal systems: Pathologies of legality.* Oxford: Oxford University Press.

Fitzpatrick, J. (1994). *Human rights in crisis: The international system for protecting rights during states of emergency* (pp. 45–46). Pennsylvania: University of Pennsylvania Press.

Harding, A. J., & Hatchard, J. (1993). Introduction. In A. J. Harding & J. Hatchard (Eds.), *Preventive detention and security law: A comparative survey* (p. 8). Boston: Martinus Nijhoff Publishers.

Hartman, J. F. (1981). Derogation from human rights treaties in public emergencies. *Harvard International Law Journal, 22*(1), 17.

Hartman, J. (1985). Working paper for the Committee of experts on the Article 4 derogation provision. *Human Rights Quarterly, 7,* 115–118.

Heap, M., & Morgans, H. (2007). Language policy and SASL: Interpreters in the public service. In W. Brian et al. (Eds.), *Disability and social change: A South African Agenda* (p. 134). Cape Town: HSRC Press.

International Commission of Jurists. (1983). *States of emergency: Their impact on human rights* 429, 430.

International Commission of Jurists. (2012). *Submission to the working group on arbitrary detention: The definition and scope of arbitrary deprivation of liberty in Customary International Law.* Available at http://icj.wpengine.netdna-cdn.com/wp-content/uploads/2012/06/Submission-working-Group-detention-analysis-brief-2012.pdf.

Iyer, V. (1999). States of emergency—Moderating their effects on human rights. *Dalhousie Law Journal, 22,* 134–135.

Kirk, J. (1997). Constitutional guarantees, characterization, and the concept of proportionality. *Melbourne University Law Review, 21,* 2.

Meron, T. (1986). *Human rights law making in the United Nations: A critique of instruments and process.* Oxford: Clarendon Press.

Office of the United Nations High Commissioner for Human Rights. (2013). *Statement of the United Nations Special Rapporteur on torture at the expert meeting on the situation of detainees held at the U.S. Naval Base at Guantanamo Bay.* Available at http://newsarchive.ohchr.org/en/NewsEvents/Pages/DisplayNews.aspx?NewsID=13859&LangID=E.

Oraa, J. (1995). *Human rights in states of emergency in International Law.* London: Clarendon Press.

Rudolph, H. (1984). The judicial review of administrative detention orders in Israel. In Y. Dinstein (Ed.), *Israel yearbook on human rights* (p. 12). Boston: Martinus Nijhoff Publishers.

U.N. Human Rights Committee. (1982). *General Comment No. 8: Right to Liberty and Security of Persons.* U.N. Doc. HRI/GEN/1/Rev.7 (June 30, 1982). Available at http://www.derechos.org/nizkor/ley/doc/obgen2en.html.

UN Commission on Human Rights. (1984). *Siracusa Principles on the Limitation and Derogation Provisions in the International Covenant on Civil and Political Rights, E/CN.4/1985/4.* Available at available at: https://www.refworld.org/docid/4672bc122.html.

UN Office of the High Commissioner for Human Rights (OHCHR). (2005). *Human Rights—A handbook for parliamentarians,* No. 8. Available at http://www.refworld.org/docid/46cea90d2.html

UN Working Group on Arbitrary Detention: Mission to Peru. (1999). *E/CN.4/199963/Add. 2.* Available at https://daccess-ods.un.org/TMP/3248046.3385582.html.

United Nations. (1949). *Commission on human rights—Summary record of the 126th meeting held at lake success,* New York, on Monday, 14 June 1949 [International Covenant on Civil and Political Rights] E/CN.4/SR. 126. See French and US alternative proposals under the Covenant, UN Doc.E/CN.4/324 (1949) and 325 (1949).

United Nations. (2003). *Human rights and arrest, pre-trial detention and administrative detention—Human rights in the administration of justice: A manual on human rights for judges, prosecutors and lawyers.* Available at http://www.ohchr.org/Documents/Publications/training9chapter5en.pdf.

United Nations Human Rights Council. (2010). *Report of the Working Group on arbitrary detention, A/HRC/13/30*. Available at https://www1.umn.edu/humanrts/wgad/2010report.pdf.
United Nations Office on Drugs And Crime. (2009). *Handbook on criminal justice, responses to terrorism*. Available at Http://Www.Unodc.Org/Documents/Terrorism/Handbook_On_Criminal_Justice_Responses_To_Terrorism_En.Pdf.
United States Senate Select Committee on Intelligence. (2012). *Committee study of the Central Intelligence Agency's detention and interrogation program: Findings and conclusions*. Available at https://www.amnestyusa.org/pdfs/sscistudy1.pdf.

Chapter 4
Preventive Detention Laws in Malaysia & Their Use

Abstract Having devised a standard preventive detention framework in Chap. 3, an attempt will be made in this Chapter, in the first instance, to use the standard framework as a yardstick to expose the weaknesses of the Malaysian Constitution's provisions concerning preventive detention. Subsequently, this Chapter will make it manifestly evident that such weaknesses have given the Parliament carte blanche to enact arbitrary laws concerning preventive detention. Consequently, it will be shown that the absence of effective safeguards in the Constitution of Malaysia has permitted succeeding generations of executives to use the extraordinary power of preventive detention in an indiscriminate manner for imposing unwarranted restrictions on the liberty of individuals.

4.1 Introduction

The historical origins of the exercise of the power of preventive detention in Malaysia, as discussed previously in Sect. 2.5, can be traced back to the British rule. Such exercise was considered an administrative necessity to deter activists of the Communist Party of Malaya (CPM), who posed dangers to the security and integrity of the state, and was sanctioned by Regulation 17 of the Emergency Regulations, 1948—promulgated during a state of emergency which was declared on 12 July 1948. The use of preventive detention to combat guerrilla communism during the British rule, subsequently, influenced the development of Malaysia's own distinctive preventive detention framework, which is contained in the Federal Constitution of Malaysia, following its emergence as an independent nation on 31 August 1957. Although the emergency of 1948 was lifted on 30 July 1960, Regulation 17 found its way into Part II of the Internal Security Act, 1960 (ISA), which was enacted by the Parliament in pursuance of Article 149(1) of the Federal Constitution to combat the threats posed by the remaining 583 armed communist terrorists in northern

---

Significantly shorter and truncated versions of this Chapter were published as Articles in the Journal of Malaysian & Comparative Law & the Suffolk Transnational Law Review (Copyright remains with the Authors) respectively.

© Springer Nature Singapore Pte Ltd. 2020
M. E. Bari, S. Naz, *The Use of Preventive Detention Laws in Malaysia: A Case for Reform*, https://doi.org/10.1007/978-981-15-5811-5_4

Peninsular.[1] Thus, a Colonial Emergency Regulation permitting the exercise of the power of preventive detention during a state of emergency was codified into a law exercisable during peace time in Malaysia. Following the repeal of the ISA in 2012 after almost 52 years of operation, new preventive detention laws, namely, the Security Offences (Special Measures) Act, 2012 (SOSMA), the Prevention of Crime Act, 1959 (PCA), as amended in 2014 and 2015, and the Prevention of Terrorism Act, 2015 (POTA), have been enacted in pursuance of Article 149(1) of the Constitution.

In this chapter, an attempt will first be made to highlight the inadequacy of the safeguards concerning preventive detention prescribed by the Constitution of Malaysia in light of the standard preventive detention framework designed in the previous chapter. Subsequently, it will be argued that the weaknesses of the constitutional provisions concerning preventive detention have permitted the enactment of a series of laws conferring wide and sweeping powers of preventive detention on the executive branch of government. The objective of these analyses is to demonstrate that due to the absence of adequate constitutional safeguards, preventive detention laws have been used by the executive to substitute the ordinary criminal laws and to silence legitimate political dissent.

4.2   The Inadequacy of the Safeguards Concerning Preventive Detention Under the Federal Constitution of Malaysia

In light of the detailed evaluation of both the provisions concerning preventive detention contained in the Malaysian Constitution in Sect. 2.6 and the safeguards that are imperative for preventing abuse of the powers of preventive detention in Sect. 3.3, an endeavour will now be made to underscore the weaknesses of the constitutional provisions concerning preventive detention.

(a) **Absence of a Guarantee Confining Preventive Detention to Formally Declared Emergencies**

Notwithstanding the necessity, as proposed by the International Commission of Jurists (ICJ) and as had been discussed in Sect. 3.3, to confine the exercise of the power of preventive detention to formally declared periods of emergency, the Malaysian Constitution does not contain any such guarantee. Rather it, as discussed earlier in Sect. 2.6.1, incorporates vague and imprecise words in Article 149 as grounds for invoking the extraordinary power of preventive detention during peacetime.

(b) **Absence of a Guarantee Requiring the Detaining Authority to Furnish the Grounds of Detention within a Specified Timeframe in Clear Terms**

---

[1] Parliamentary Debates: Dewan Rakyat (House of Representatives), 21 June 1960.

The stipulation of a specific timeframe in the Constitution, as discussed earlier in Sect. 3.3., obligating the detaining authority to furnish the grounds of detention, which are sufficiently detailed and are also expressed in clear terms, to an individual kept in preventive custody facilitates his right to make an effective representation against the detention order. However, notwithstanding the utility of such a guarantee, Article 151(1)(a) of the Malaysian Constitution, as discussed in Sect. 2.6.1(c), neither specifies a timeframe within which the detainee should be informed of the grounds of detention nor obliges the detaining authority to ensure that the grounds supplied are sufficiently detailed and are couched in clear language.

(c) **Absence of a Guarantee Permitting the Detainee to Make a Representation within a Specified Timeframe**

Although permitting the detainee to make a representation against his detention before an independent Advisory Body, as discussed earlier in Sect. 3.3, within the shortest possible time provides an opportunity for him to convince the Board that his detention is not necessary for dealing with the threats posed to the security of the nation, the Malaysian Constitution stipulates that an individual can be detained for 3 months without the concurrence of the Board. Furthermore, unlike the Constitution of Pakistan, the Malaysian Constitution, as discussed earlier in Sect. 2.6.1(c), neither authorises the head of the judiciary to constitute the Advisory Board nor confines the membership of such a Board solely to individuals who are or have been judges of the superior courts for preventing the executive from adversely influencing the functioning of the Board. Rather the Malaysian Constitution authorises the executive to not only constitute the Board but also to choose its composition.

(d) **Denial of the Right of a Detainee to Challenge the Legality of Detention Order**

The right to challenge the legality of a detention order in pursuance of a writ of *habeas corpus* is one of the core safeguards against arbitrary detention. The judiciary in turn should decide the matter expeditiously and subsequently order the release of the detainee if the detention is found to be unlawful.[2] Notwithstanding the utility of such a guarantee, the Malaysian Constitution, as pointed out earlier in Sect. 2.6.1(b), does not extend to anyone deprived of his liberty under a preventive detention law a right to challenge the lawfulness of his detention order. Rather the Constitution specifically stipulates in Article 149(1) that laws concerning preventive detention can, among other things, be inconsistent with the guarantees contained in Article 5, including the right of a detainee to challenge the legality of his detention order.

(e) **Absence of a Guarantee Barring Detention Incommunicado**

Detention incommunicado, as discussed earlier in Sect. 3.2.1(a), makes it easier for detaining authorities to subject individuals kept in preventive custody to torture, cruel, inhuman or degrading treatment. However, Article 149(1) of the Malaysian Constitution, as pointed out earlier in Sect. 2.6.1(b), instead of

---

[2] Cook H. (1992), p. 25.

stipulating a guarantee against detaining individuals incommunicado, specifically deprives a detainee, among other things, the right to consult and to be defended by a lawyer. Furthermore, the Constitution does not contain any provision enabling a detainee to communicate with his family members.

(f) **Absence of a Prohibition on Indefinite Detention**

It should be reiterated here that investing the executive, as pointed out earlier in Sects. 3.2.1 and 3.3(d), with the authority to detain an individual for an indefinite period of time permits the disturbing possibility of facilitating the torture of detainees. However, the Constitution of Malaysia, as discussed earlier in Sect. 2.6.3(d), does not fix the maximum period for keeping an individual in preventive custody.

(g) **Absence of a Provision Concerning Monetary Compensation**

When the constitution of a nation, as pointed out earlier in Sect. 3.3, contains a provision for monetary compensation in cases of gross abuse of the power of preventive detention, it has the beneficial effect of persuading the executive to refrain from arbitrarily detaining an astounding number of individuals. Taking into account the utility of such a guarantee, the ICCPR in Article 9(5), as pointed out earlier in Sect. 3.2.1(e), extends victims of arbitrary detention a right to monetary compensation. However, it should be stressed here that the Malaysian Constitution does not extend such a guarantee to those who have been arbitrarily deprived of their liberty. Furthermore, Malaysia is one of the 16 nations which has neither signed nor ratified the ICCPR.[3]

4.3   Evaluation of the Provisions Concerning Preventive Detention in the ISA, SOSMA, PCA and POTA

Having identified the weaknesses of the constitutional provisions concerning preventive detention, an attempt will now be made to: a) analyse the purpose behind the enactment of the ISA, SOSMA, PCA and POTA; and b) examine the provisions concerning preventive detention and procedural safeguards available to detainees under these laws.

---

[3] International Covenant on Civil and Political Rights (ICCPR), opened for signature on 16 December 1966, 999 UNTS 171 (entered into force on 23 March 1976).

4.3.1 The Internal Security Act, 1960 (ISA) and the Purpose Behind Its Enactment

The Malayan Emergency of 1948, as mentioned earlier in Sect. 4.1, was lifted in 1960. However, the Malaysian Government was still apprehensive of the threats posed by the communists to the safety and security of the nascent nation. Consequently, the ISA became the first law, which was passed in pursuance of Article 149(1) of the Federal Constitution, in independent Malaysia to empower the executive to exercise the power of preventive detention. In moving the second reading of the ISA Bill in the Parliament on 21 June 1960, the then Deputy Prime Minister, Tun Abdul Razak, explained the rationale for the enactment of the ISA in the following words:

> The Hon'ble Prime Minister and other Members of the Government, including myself, have made it quite clear on a number of occasions that, because the Emergency is to be declared at an end, the Government does not intend to relax its vigilance against the evil enemy who still remains as a threat on our border and who is now attempting by subversion to succeed where he has failed by force of arms. It is for this reason that this Bill is before the House. It has two main aims: firstly to counter subversion throughout the country and, secondly, to enable the necessary measures to be taken on the border area to counter terrorism.[4]

The long title of the ISA stated that the purpose of the Act was "to provide for the internal security of Malaysia, preventive detention, the prevention of subversion, the suppression of organised violence against persons and property in specific areas of Malaysia and for matters incidental thereto". The ISA was expected to be a temporary measure aimed at suppressing the communist subversion, as is evident from the following observations of RH Hickling, a British jurist and the drafter of the ISA: "I must hope that the practice of imprisonment without trial, charge or conviction admitted by the Act, 1960 will not be regarded as a permanent feature of the legal and political landscape of Malaya".[5] The exigency which warranted the enactment of the ISA in 1960 ceased to exist after the conclusion of a treaty between the Malaysian Government and the CPM in Bangkok on 24 December 1989.[6] However, notwithstanding the cessation of the hostilities, the ISA was allowed to remain in force.

Subsequently, the Supreme Court of Malaysia in the case of *Theresa Lim Chin Chin v. Inspector General of Police*[7] opined that the use of the ISA was not limited to the detention of communists. However, the counsel for the appellants in this case submitted that the application of the ISA by dint of Article 149(1) of the Constitution was limited to combatting communist insurgency and subversion. In support of this assertion, he argued that the terms of Article 149(1) require any law passed to stop or prevent action which has been taken or threatened by a substantial body of

---

[4] Parliamentary Debates, Dewan Rakyat (House of Representatives) June 21, 1960, p. 1185.
[5] Hickling (1962), p. 183.
[6] Yatim (1995), p. 293.
[7] *Theresa Lim Chin Chin v. Inspector General of Police* [1988] 1 MLJ 293.

persons, must be limited in its application to prevent "that action" only. He further referred to the observations of the Reid Commission, as discussed earlier in Sect. 2.6, when recommending the insertion of Article 149 in the Constitution. The Commission in its observations, among other things, had stressed the importance of limiting the Parliament's ability to "authorize infringement" of fundamental rights by laws only to the extent necessary to prevent "violence against persons or property".[8] Finally, the counsel made reference to Deputy Prime Minister Razak's speech in the Parliament, as discussed above, asserting that the ISA was enacted to counter the "subversion" and "terrorism" perpetrated by the communists.

However, Lord President Salleh Abas—the then head of the judiciary—discounted the importance of the Reid Commission Report and the speech of the Deputy Prime Minister while interpreting the ISA. He observed that they were only relevant for appreciating "the legislative history of an Act, and … [as such they] cannot be regarded as the basis or the determining factor for interpreting the Act or any provision of the Act… [Otherwise] the court will cease to be the ultimate interpreters of law because in the end what is law will be guided by what the politicians said in Parliament" or what was recommended by the Reid Commission.[9] Consequently, the learned judge concluded that "there…[was] nothing to show [from the wording of the provision of the ISA] that it… [was] restricted to communist activities".[10]

The Federal Court also reiterated the above observations of the Supreme Court in *Mohd Ezam Mohd Noor v. Ketua Polis Negara & Other Appeals*,[11] when it observed that there is nothing in Article 149 of the Federal Constitution or in the ISA that could support the interpretation that the latter was limited in its application to only deal with the threats posed by the communists.[12]

Thus, it is evident that an extraordinary law concerning preventive detention, which was enacted for deterring communist insurgency, became a tool for the government to use during peacetime.

4.3.1.1 The Provisions Concerning Preventive Detention Under the ISA

The ISA in its recital reproduced the first sentence of Article 149(1), i.e. "[w]hereas action has been taken …", and subsequently included paragraphs (a) and (d) of this Article, i.e. "to cause, and to cause a substantial number of citizens to fear, organised violence against persons and property; and … to procure the alteration, otherwise than by lawful means, of the lawful government of Malaysia by law

---

[8] Final Report of Federation of Malaya Constitutional Commission (Reid Commission) (1957), Chapter IX Fundamental Rights – Emergency Powers, para174.

[9] *Theresa Lim Chin Chin v. Inspector General of Police* [1988] 1 MLJ 293, 296.

[10] Ibid.

[11] *Mohd Ezam Mohd Noor v. Ketua Polis Negara & Other Appeals* [2002] 4 CLJ 309, 360.

[12] Ibid.

established".[13] Thus, it fulfilled the only condition precedent for the enactment of a statute in pursuance of Article 149.[14] The power of preventive detention under the ISA was provided for by two sections, namely sections 8 and 73. An attempt will now be made to examine these provisions concerning preventive detention.

4.3.1.1.1   The Power of Preventive Detention Under Section 8 of the ISA

Article 149(1) of the Malaysian Constitution, as pointed out earlier in Sect. 2.6.2, uses vague and broad terms for the enactment of preventive detention laws. Consequently, the laws passed in pursuance of this Article contain ambiguous and all-embracing words as grounds warranting the exercise of the extraordinary power of preventive detention.

The ISA in section 8(1) authorized the Minister of Home Affairs to order the detention of a person on the basis of his satisfaction that the person was acting in a manner "prejudicial to the security or prejudicial to the maintenance of essential services or prejudicial to the economic life of Malaysia". The words, "prejudicial to the security or prejudicial to the maintenance of essential services or prejudicial to the economic life of Malaysia", as used in the ISA were neither defined in the Act nor were there any list or examples provided by it for clarifying which activities could constitute threats to the security of the nation. Rather the Home Minister was given the unfettered discretion to determine whether an individual had acted in a manner prejudicial to the security of the nation. Furthermore, the Malaysian judiciary in preventive detention cases under the ISA refused to give section 8(1) an objective interpretation, i.e., an interpretation which would have enabled it to examine the validity of a detention order by asking for the facts relating to the grounds which satisfied the Minister to issue such an order. Instead, it embraced a subjective interpretation, thereby deferring to the executive contention of what would constitute a threat to security and consequently warrant the exercise of the power of preventive detention. This position was first articulated by the Federal Court—now the highest court of law in Malaysia—in *Karam Singh v. Menteri Hal Ehwal Dalam Negeri (Minister of Home Affairs)*, which concerned detention of an individual under the ISA on vague and insufficient grounds.[15] Suffian FJ (as he then was) held that:

> Whether or not the facts on which the order of detention is to be based are sufficient or relevant, is a matter to be decided solely by the executive. In making their decision, they

---

[13] The ISA's recital provided "Whereas action has been taken and further action is threatened by a substantial body of person both inside and outside Malaysia:- 1) to cause, and to cause a substantial number of citizens to fear, organised violence against persons and property; and 2) to procure the alteration, otherwise than by lawful means, of the lawful government of Malaysia by law established.
AND WHEREAS the action taken and threatened is prejudicial to the security of Malaysia. AND WHEREAS Parliament considers it necessary to stop or prevent that action."

[14] *Teh Cheng Poh v. Public Prosecutor* [1979] 1 MLJ 50 at p. 54.

[15] *Karam Singh v. Menteri Hal Ehwal Dalam Negeri (Minister of Home Affairs)* [1969] 2 MLJ 129.

have complete discretion and it is not for a court of law to question the sufficiency or relevance of these allegations of fact.[16]

It is evident from the above observations that Suffian FJ in adopting a subjective interpretation was influenced by the subjective interpretation test as had been adopted by the majority of the judges of the House of Lords in the infamous case of *Liversidge v. Anderson.*[17] In this case, the appellant—Mr. Robert Liversidge—was detained during World War II under an order issued by the Home Secretary pursuant to Regulation 18B of the Defence (General) Regulations 1939, which permitted the Secretary to order the detention of an individual if he had "reasonable cause to believe" that such an individual was of "hostile origin or associations or to have been concerned in acts prejudicial to the public safety or the defence of the realm". The House of Lords by a majority of four to one (Lord Atkin dissenting) held that "the grounds on which the Secretary of State" could "make his order of detention" was left to his sole discretion, which subsequently could not be called into question in a court of law.[18] However, Lord Atkin in his famous dissent in *Liversidge* observed that both the common law and the rules of statutory construction dictate that judges are authorized to examine the grounds on which the executive exercises its power to detain an individual so as to determine whether the power has been exercised objectively. His Lordship also lamented the fact that his colleagues paid undue deference to the executive at the expense of the liberty of individuals. As he remarked:

I view with apprehension the attitude of judges who on a mere question of construction, when face to face with claims involving the liberty of the subject, show themselves more executive-minded than the executive… It has always been one of the pillars of freedom, one of the principles of liberty for which on recent authority we are now fighting, that the judges are no respecters of persons and stand between the subject and any attempted encroachments on his liberty by the executive, alert to see that any coercive action is justified in law.[19]

Notwithstanding the subsequent endorsement of the objective interpretation test propounded by Lord Atkin in a series of cases in Britain,[20] the Malaysian judiciary continued to choose the subjective interpretation as its preferred interpretive technique for dealing with preventive detention cases under the ISA. For instance, in *Re Tan Sri Raja Khalid bin Raja Raja Harun; Inspector-General of Police v Tan Sri Raja Khalid bin,*[21] the Supreme Court, which was the highest court of the land until 1994, held that:

[T]he detaining authorities are not obliged to disclose the facts which led them to so believe nor are they required to prove in court the sufficiency or adequacy of the reasons for such belief in any proceedings for habeas corpus instituted by the detainee. It is sufficient if the

---

[16] Ibid., p. 151.

[17] *Liversidge v. Anderson* [1942] AC 206.

[18] Ibid., pp. 221–222.

[19] Ibid., 244.

[20] *Her Majesty's Treasury v. Ahmad, etc,* [2010] UKSC 2, para 6.

[21] *Re Tan Sri Raja Khalid bin Raja Raja Harun; Inspector-General of Police v Tan Sri Raja Khalid bin* (1988) 1 MLJ 182.

detaining authorities show that the person has been detained in exercise of a valid legal power... where the detaining authorities invoke national security as the grounds for non-disclosure of facts leading to the making of an order of detention, the test to be applied by the court in any proceedings for habeas corpus would be a subjective test. The court cannot in those circumstances compel the disclosure of such facts.[22]

4.3.1.1.2   The Power of Preventive Detention Under Section 73 of the ISA

Unlike section 8(1) of the ISA, which authorised the Home Minister to exercise the power of preventive detention, section 73(1) empowered any police officer to preventively detain an individual pending inquiry if the former had reason to believe:

(a) that there ... [were] grounds which would justify detention of the detainee under s. 8; and
(b) that the detainee... [had] acted or ... [was] about to act or ... [was] likely to act in any manner prejudicial to the security of Malaysia or any part thereof or to the maintenance of essential services therein or to the economic life thereof.

Thus, it is evident from a perusal of the provision contained in Section 73(1) that police officers were also granted the unconstrained discretion to exercise the power of preventive detention on broad and vague grounds. The only restriction to the issuance of an order of detention under section 73(1) against an individual was that such a power could not be used if a similar order had already been issued against him under section 8. As to whether a subjective or an objective test had to be applied in reviewing the legality of detention orders issued under Section 73(1), the Malaysian Judiciary initially favoured a subjective test, as is evident from the decision of the Supreme Court—then the final court of appeal—in 1988 in the case of *Inspector General of Police v. Tan Sri Raja Khalid bin Raja Harun.*[23] The Supreme Court held: "Section 73(1) and section 8 of the ISA are so inextricably connected that the subjective test should be applied to both. The court cannot require the police officer to prove to the court the sufficiency of the reason for his belief under s. 73(1)."[24]

However, 14 years later, the Federal Court—the current highest court of the nation—in *Mohamad Ezam Mohd Noor v. Ketua Polis Negara,*[25] refused to follow the above precedent established by its predecessor. Rather it held that the test to be applied for interpreting the reasons for issuing an order of detention under Section 73(1) of ISA would be an objective one. As Chief Justice Steve Shim observed:

I take the view that as the arrest and a detention by the police officer entail the curtailment of the liberty of a subject involving, as I have said, a basic and fundamental right, his exercise of discretion under s. 73(1) is therefore subject to the objective test and thus reviewable by a court of law. The decision of the police is objectively justiciable. This means that the

---

[22] Ibid.
[23] *Inspector General of Police v. Tan Sri Raja Khalid bin Raja Harun* [1988] 1 CLJ 39.
[24] *Inspector General of Police v. Tan Sri Raja Khalid bin Raja Harun* [1988] 1 CLJ 39, 140.
[25] *Mohamad Ezam Mohd Noor v. Ketua Polis Negara* [2002] 4 CLJ 309.

question whether a police officer has the required "reason to believe" when he makes the arrest and detention in reliance on s. 73(1) is objectively justiciable. The burden is on the police officer to satisfy the court that the preconditions constituting the said section which set out the jurisdictional threshold requisite to the exercise of arrest and detention have been complied with.[26]

Thus, it is evident from the decision of the Federal Court that courts were entitled to review the sufficiency and reasonableness of the reasons which led the police to conclude under section 73(1) of the ISA that the detained individual was about to act in a manner prejudicial to the security of Malaysia. However, the conflicting judgments pronounced by the Federal Court and its predecessor in the above cases aroused doubts about the test applicable to Section 73(1). The Federal Court provided some clarity regarding the issue when it observed in the case of *Dalip Bhagwan Singh v. Public Prosecutor*[27] that:

> In Malaysia, the Federal Court and its forerunner i.e., Supreme Court, after all appeals to the Privy Council were abolished, has never refused to depart from its own decision when it appeared right to do so....it has indeed and in practice been followed, though such power to depart from its own previous decision has been exercised sparingly also....When two decisions of the Federal Court conflict, on a point of law, the later decision therefore, for the same reasons [its decision represents the present state of law], prevails over the earlier decision.[28]

In light of the above the decision of the Federal Court in *Dalip Bhagwan*, it can be concluded that the courts could adopt an objective test for examining the grounds relied on by a police officer under section 73(1) of the ISA for preventively detaining an individual.

4.3.1.1.3   Maximum Period of Preventive Detention Under the ISA

The Constitution of Malaysia, as pointed out earlier in Sect. 2.6.3(c), does not prescribe a maximum period of preventive detention, which in turn provides the Parliament carte blanche power to prescribe by law the maximum period of preventive detention. An attempt will now be made to examine the period of detention fixed by sections 8 and 73. First, section 8(1) of the ISA empowered the Home Minister to detain an individual for a period not exceeding 2 years. However, Section 8(7) authorised the Minister to extend the period of detention for a period not exceeding 2 years at a time.[29] Thus, section 8(7) allowed the detention of a person for an indefinite period of time as this provision prescribed no time limit to the number of times the executive could extend a detention order. Consequently, these

---

[26] *Mohamad Ezam Mohd Noor v. Ketua Polis Negara* [2002] 4 CLJ 309, 342.

[27] *Dalip Bhagwan Singh v. Public Prosecutor* [1997] 4 CLJ 645.

[28] *Dalip Bhagwan Singh v. Public Prosecutor* [1997] 4 CLJ 645, 661–662.

[29] Section 8(7) of the ISA stated that, "The Minister may direct that the duration of any detention order or restriction order be extended for such further period, not exceeding 2 years, as he may specify, and thereafter for such further periods, not exceeding 2 years at a time, as he may specify."

wide powers were indiscriminately used to detain political adversaries for a prolonged period notwithstanding the adverse impact of such detention on the fundamental human rights of individuals, such as the right not to be subjected to torture. For instance, R. Gunaratnam, who was an ordinary member of the People's Party of Malaysia, was preventively detained under the ISA on 14 November 1970. It was alleged that the detainee had been involved in communist activities. Gunaratnam was kept in preventive custody for 11 years and 8 months until July 1982.[30]

In the same vein, S. N. Rajah, who was the executive secretary of the United Malayan Estate Workers, was detained for 11 years and 2 months beginning from 1970 to 1981. However, unlike Gunaratnam, he was alleged to have been involved in activities "prejudicial to the security of the Federation".[31]

Furthermore, certain opposition political party members were kept in preventive custody for even longer periods. For instance, Tan Hock Hin, who was a former Socialist Front legislator for one of the constituencies in Penang, was detained under the ISA for 15 years from 1967 to 1982.[32] However, the longest period for which an individual was preventively detained under the ISA was a staggering 16 years. The name of this individual was Loo Ming Liong and he was allegedly detained on the suspicion of being a communist.[33] It seems evidently incongruous for the purposes of combating communism to detain individuals for prolonged periods such as 16 years.

Even academicians were not kept outside the purview of the wide powers of the ISA. For instance, Syed Husin Ali—a Professor of Sociology at the University of Malaya, which is the nation's premier university—was detained for almost 6 years on the suspicion that he was "involved willingly and knowingly in an attempt to overthrow the government by force and for cooperating with the communists".[34]

It should be stressed here that the objective underlying the exercise of the power of preventive detention under the ISA was to prevent the commission of activities prejudicial to the security of the nation. However, the use of such power to detain individuals, as discussed above, for a prolonged period of time was manifestly disproportionate to the purpose of safeguarding the security of the nation.

Second, section 73(3) of the ISA initially empowered a police officer to preventively detaine an individual for a maximum period of 30 days. However, the Internal Security (Amendment) Act, 1971 increased the period for which a police officer could detain an individual from 30 to 60 days. The Explanatory Statement accompanying the Bill for the 1971 Amendment Act stated that the decision to increase the period for which an individual could be detained was made due to "difficulties

---

[30] See above n 6, p. 259.

[31] Ibid.

[32] Ibid., p. 69.

[33] Ibid.

[34] Ibid.

which… [had] arisen in practice".[35] From the Parliamentary Debates preceding the enactment of the Amendment Act of 1971, it became evident that the practical difficulties referred to in the Explanatory Statement to the Bill was the apparent insufficiency of the period of 30 days for transferring the files of a person detained under section 73(1) from the detaining police officer to the Police Headquarters and ultimately to the Minister of Home Affairs.[36] It should be stressed here that the ISA remained in force until 2012 and, as such, it can be argued that the reasons for extending the period of detention under section 73(3) could no longer be said to be applicable in the later stages of the life of the Act "given the advancement in telecommunication and transportation technology".[37]

There were also instances of undue deprivation of liberty under section 73 of the ISA. For instance, Raja Petra Raja Kamaruddin, who is the Editor of Malaysia Today and was one of the architects of the campaign to free Anwar Ibrahim—the former Deputy Prime Minister of Malaysia—was detained under section 73(1) of the ISA and was released on the 52nd day of his detention. Upon release, he testified before the SUHAKAM Open Inquiry on the ISA that in his case all the questions asked by the Police during interrogation had been answered and subsequently everything had been documented within the 30th day of the detention. Consequently, Raja Petra claimed that for the next 22 days of his detention, he was kept in detention because the Police had the power to keep him for another 30 days and not because such detention was necessary for safeguarding the security of the nation.[38] This assertion of Raja Petra is bolstered by the decisions of the Malaysian Courts in cases, such as *Abdul Ghani Haroon v. Ketua Polis Negara* and *Nasharuddin Nasir v. Kerajaan Malaysia & Ors.* In both cases, the Court held that it was not necessary for the police to extend the period of detention of individuals kept in preventive custody under section 73 of the ISA. However, the police nevertheless extended such periods of detention without proper application of mind.[39]

4.3.1.1.4 Safeguards Provided to the Detainee Under the ISA

The Federation Constitution of Malaysia, as discussed earlier in Sect. 2.6.3(c), in Article 151 provides certain safeguards to individuals kept in preventive custody, which in the absence of any specific exclusion clause in the Constitution should be read into the laws concerning preventive detention and should be available to any person detained under the security laws passed in accordance with the Constitution. The Constitution, as pointed out earlier in Sect. 2.6.3(b), in Article 5 also stipulates

[35] Human Rights Commission of Malaysia (2003), p. 37, http://www.suhakam.org.my/wp-content/uploads/2013/12/review-of-the-ISA-1960.pdf
[36] Parliamentary Debates, Dewan Rakyat, July 30, 1971, p. 4095.
[37] See above n 35.
[38] See above n 35, 38.
[39] *Abdul Ghani Haroon v. Ketua Polis Negara* [2001] 2 MLJ 689 and *Nasharuddin Nasir v. Kerajaan Malaysia & Ors (No. 2)* [2003] 1 CLJ 353.

certain guarantees to detainees. However, Article 149(1) of the Constitution, as discussed earlier in Sect. 2.6.3(b), enables preventive detention laws to be inconsistent with the guarantees contained in Article 5. An attempt will now be made to evaluate the safeguards that had been provided to detainees under the ISA.

(a) **Rights to be Defended by a Legal Practitioner and to be Informed of the Grounds of Detention**

Article 5(3) of the Federal Constitution of Malaysia provides two types of rights to individuals deprived of his liberty. One of these is the right to be defended by a legal practitioner of one's choice. However, the Constitution, as pointed out earlier in Sect. 2.6.3(b), authorizes preventive detention laws to be inconsistent with, among other things, this right guaranteed by Article 5(3). Accordingly, the ISA did not afford this safeguard to detainees.

Perhaps taking into account the utility of the above right for an individual kept in preventive custody to facilitate an effective representation against the order of detention, the High Court in *Borhan Hj Daud & Ors v. Abd Malek Hussin*[40] forcefully observed that the exercise of the power of preventive detention under the ISA would be vitiated by *mala fide* if the detaining authority did not afford the detainee, among other things, the right to counsel during his detention.[41] But when the government challenged the decision, the Court of Appeal adopted an overtly formalist reasoning and overturned the decision of the High Court. For the Court of Appeal held that.

[T]he ISA... is a special law which is valid even though it contains provisions inconsistent with the provisions on fundamental liberties under the Constitution... [D]etention under the ISA does not require the detaining authority to disclose material evidence and sufficient particulars as to the reasons for his arrest and further detention. Even in ordinary law, it is not a requirement for the arresting authority to state the offence or charge in technical and precise language. Thus, the question of mala fide has not been substantiated....We hold that a violation of art. 5(3) i.e., right to access to counsel does not make the arrest and detention mala fide.[42]

It is pertinent to note here that Article 151(1)(a) of Federal Constitution, as discussed earlier in Sect. 2.6.3(c), also obligates the detaining authority to communicate the grounds of detention to an individual kept in preventive custody. However, the Constitution through the use of the words "as soon as may be" does not specify a timeframe within which such grounds should be communicated to the detainee. Taking advantage of this lacuna in the Constitution, section 11(2)(b)(i) of the ISA also kept the timeframe for informing the grounds of detention to an individual detained under section 8 indeterminate. However, no obligation was imposed on the detaining authority to communicate such grounds if an individual was preventively detained under section 73 of the ISA.

---

[40] *Borhan Hj Daud & Ors v. Abd Malek Hussin* [2010] 8 CLJ 656.
[41] Ibid.
[42] *Borhan Hj Daud & Ors v. Abd Malek Hussin* [2010] 8 CLJ 656, 674.

Furthermore, with regard to the issue of extending the period of detention under section 8(7) of the ISA, the Federal Court in the case of *Gurcharan Singh Bachittar Singh v. Penguasa, Tempat Tahanan Perlindungan Kamunting, Taiping & Ors*[43] brought to light a peculiarity in the application of the Act. For it would appear from the decision of the Court in this case that the only detainees entitled to the grounds of detention under section 11(2)(b)(i) of the ISA were those: a) whose detention orders were extended on grounds different from those contained in the original orders; and b) whose detention order were extended partly on the same and partly on different grounds.[44] Thus, detainees who were detained for a further period on the same grounds as the initial order were not entitled to such statements.[45]

(b) Right to Make a Representation before the Advisory Board

It may be recalled from the discussion in Sect. 2.6.3(c) that Article 151(1)(b) of the Constitution, as amended in 1960 and 1976 respectively, provides that an individual can be kept in preventive custody for an indefinite period of time without the concurrence of an Advisory Board. However, Section 11(1) read together with Section 12(1) of the ISA stipulated that an individual could not be preventively detained for a period longer than 3 months without being afforded the opportunity to make a representation against his detention order before an Advisory Board. However, the effectiveness of this safeguard was undermined by the fact that the recommendation put forward by the Advisory Board was not binding on the Yang di Pertuan Agong (YDPA)—the head of the state. Thus, the YDPA was given the unfettered discretion under the ISA to ignore the recommendation of the Board when deciding whether a detainee should be released. Moreover, section 12(2) of the ISA made it manifestly clear that such a decision of the YDPA regarding the fate of the detainee was final and could not be called into question in any court of law.

(c) Access to Judicial Review

Article 5(2) of the Federal Constitution reads as follows:
Where complaint is made to a High Court or any judge thereof that a person is being unlawfully detained the court shall inquire into the complaint and unless satisfied that the detention is lawful, shall order him to be produced before the court and release him.

Justice Hishamudin in the case of *Abdul Ghani Haroon v. Ketua Polis Negara & Anor,*[46] highlighted the importance of this guarantee stipulated by Article 5(2) of the Constitution in the following manner:

by virtue of cl.(2) of art.5 of the Federal Constitution…the right to apply to the High Court for a writ of *habeas corpus* was not merely a legal right, but also a constitutional right available to any person who believes that he has been unlawfully detained.[47]

---

[43] *Gurcharan Singh Bachittar Singh v. Penguasa, Tempat Tahanan Perlindungan Kamunting, Taiping & Ors* [2002] 4 MLJU 255.

[44] See above n 35, p. 75.

[45] See above n 35, p. 75.

[46] *Abdul Ghani Haroon v. Ketua Polis Negara & Anor* [2001] 2 MLJ 689.

[47] Ibid., p. 696.

The utility of the writ of *habeas corpus* for individuals kept in preventive custody was further explained by Durga Das Basu—a noted Indian Jurist—in the following terms:

> The object of issuing the writ is to ascertain whether there is any legal justification for the detention of the person in custody. The merit of the case or the moral justification for imprisoning the petitioner is no relevant consideration in a proceeding for *habeas corpus*. Thus, a person charged with treason or murder is entitled to be set at liberty, if his imprisonment has not taken place in due course of law. A detention, thus, becomes unlawful not only where there is no law to justify it but also where procedure prescribed by the law which authorises the detention has not been followed, and, in determining whether such procedure has been complied with, the Court applies a strict standard, not only in interpreting the terms of the statute but also in exacting a strict compliance with the requirements, so interpreted, in fact.[48]

Perhaps taking into account the above realities, the original section 8 of the ISA afforded detainees the right to judicial review. However, in order to make the ISA consistent with the terms of the proviso to Article 149(1) of the Constitutions of Malaysia, which, among other things, permits preventive detentions laws to exclude the authority of the judiciary to question the legality of preventive detention orders, this safeguard was dispensed with by the government of the day through the enactment of the Internal Security (Amendment) Act, 1989. Mahathir Mohamad—the then Prime Minister—while tabling the Internal Security (Amendment Act) made the following observations:

> The interventionist role of judicial decisions and the trends of foreign courts should not be copied because such actions … [were] against the concept of separation of powers between the executive and the judiciary which was upheld in Malaysia. If the courts can reverse executive's decision, it would make it impossible for the executive to make any decision for fear that the courts would intervene. The ruling party would then be waiting for the decisions of the courts and the results of appeal to higher courts.[49]

In line with the Prime Minister's contemptuous attitude towards the judiciary, as manifested before the Parliament, the Explanatory Statement accompanying the Bill for the Internal Security (Amendment) Act 1989, explained the rationale of the amendment in the following manner:

> This provision is necessary to avoid any possibility of the courts substituting their judgment of that of the Executive in matters concerning security of the country… In matters of national security and public order, it is clearly the Executive which is the best authority to make evaluations of available information in order to decide on precautionary measures to be taken and to have a final say in such matters; not the courts which have to depend on proof of evidence.[50]

Thus, it is evident from the above explanations put forward by the then Prime Minister and the Parliament that the amendments were purposefully incorporated in the ISA to limit the power of judicial review as the judiciary in some

---

[48] Basu and Nandi (2000), p. 544.

[49] Hector (2006), http://www.malaysianbar.org.my/human_rights/detention_without_trial_laws_in_malaysia_.html

[50] See above n 35, 81.

cases had stood between the executive and the arbitrary encroachment on the liberty of individuals.

Section 8C of the ISA, which was inserted by the Internal Security (Amendment) Act, 1989, specified that "judicial review" for the purposes of the ISA not only included proceedings instituted by way of a writ of *habeas corpus* but also applications for *mandamus, prohibition, certiorari,* injunction and any "suit or action or other legal proceedings relating to or arising out of any act done or decision made by the Yang di-Pertuan Agong or the Minister in accordance with the Act". Having clarified the meaning of the term "judicial review" for the purposes of the Act, the newly inserted ouster clause, i.e. Section 8B(1), restricted the judiciary's power to review Ministerial detention order on substantive grounds in the following manner:

There shall be no judicial review in any court of and no court shall have or exercise any jurisdiction in respect of, any act done or decision made by the Yang di Pertuan Agong or the Minister in the exercise of their discretionary power in accordance with this Act, save in regard to any question or compliance with any procedural requirement in this Act governing such act or decision.

Consequently, the judiciary adopted an overly formalistic interpretation of the above ouster clause when asked to review detention orders passed by the government under the ISA. For instance, in *Kerajaan Malaysia & Ors. v. Nasharuddin Nasir,*[51] the Federal Court adopted such an approach in interpreting the effect of the ouster clause contained in section 8B of the ISA. In this context, the observations of Chief Justice Steve Shim are noteworthy:

In my view, the words in s. 8B are explicit. They are clear and precise. They are exclusionary in nature and effect. The intention of Parliament is unmistakably obvious i.e., that the jurisdiction of the court is to be ousted in terms stated in s. 8B. In the premises… the court must give expression to Parliament's intention. Section 8B is therefore intended to exclude judicial review by the court of any act done or any decision made by the Minister in the exercise of his discretionary power in accordance with the ISA except as regards any question on compliance with any procedural requirement relating to the act or decision in question.[52]

Thus, it is evident that the Federal Court in interpreting the ouster clause contained in the ISA did leave a small window of opportunity open for courts to examine detention orders when the facts revealed that the detaining authority did not comply with the procedural requirements under the Act. This stance had been reaffirmed by the Federal Court in two other cases. For instance, the Court in *Ng Boon Hock v. Penguasa, Tempat Tahanan Perlindungan Kamunting, Taiping & Ors,*[53] held:

---

[51] *Kerajaan Malaysia & Ors. v. Nasharuddin Nasir* [2004] 1 CLJ 81.

[52] *Kerajaan Malaysia & Ors. v. Nasharuddin Nasir* [2004] 1 CLJ 81, 93, 95.

[53] *Ng Boon Hock v. Penguasa, Tempat Tahanan Perlindungan Kamunting, Taiping & Ors* [1998] MLJ 174

As can be clearly seen, the term 'judicial review' as defined in section 8C encompasses almost every action that can be taken to court. The usage of the word 'includes' clearly indicates that the list of items of 'judicial review' in the said section is not exhaustive. Hence, reading section 8B together with section 8C of the said Act, the only action anyone can take to court for any offence under the said Act is 'in regard to any question on compliance with any procedural requirement in this Act governing such act of decision'. This means that one can only challenge the act done or decision made by the Yang di-Pertuan Agong [the King] or the Minister on a question of non-compliance with any procedural requirement governing such act or decision.[54]

In *Abdul Razak bin Baharuddin & Ors v. Ketua Polis Negara & Ors and another appeal*,[55] Abdul Hamid Mohamad FCJ held that:

We reiterate now that this court must give effect to the provisions of ss. 8B, 8C... It means, inter alia, that an order of the Minister under s. 8 may only be challenged on the ground of procedural non-compliance ... We shall now summarize our discussion in one sentence: a detention order made under s. 8 of the ISA may only be challenged on the ground of procedural non-compliance and nothing else.[56]

As to what would be construed as procedural requirements under the ISA, the High Court in *Raja Petra Raja Kamarudin v. Menteri Hal Ehwal Dalam Negeri*[57] observed:

What then are the procedural requirements in the Act? There is a dearth of procedural requirements in relation to making a detention order under s. 8 of the Act. Certainly nothing in the Act goes in the way of expressly referring to matters therein as procedural requirements. But regardless, as the preamble is to be construed and have effect as part of the an Act pursuant to s. 15 of the Interpretation Act 1948 & 1967, there is merit in the contention that those matters in the preamble which are matters preliminary to the exercise of jurisdiction under the Act ought to come within the scope of what is termed in s. 8B as "procedural requirement". The Federal Courts in all ... [the previous] cases ... have clearly settled that the exercise of discretion under s. 8 of the Act may only be reviewed on the ground of procedural non-compliance ... [However], the procedural requirements of the Act have not been exhaustively defined in the Act or by the case law.[58]

In light of the above decision, it is evident that in the absence of any express guidelines contained in the ISA as to its procedural requirement, the High Court observed that it would be a procedural requirement for the Minister to exercise the power of preventive detention in accordance with the objectives enumerated in the preamble of the Act.[59] The Court further held:

---

[54] *Ng Boon Hock v. Penguasa, Tempat Tahanan Perlindungan Kamunting, Taiping & Ors* [1998] MLJ 174,178.

[55] *Abdul Razak bin Baharuddin & Ors v. Ketua Polis Negara & Ors and another appeal* [2005] 4 CLJ 445.

[56] Ibid., pp. 453, 455.

[57] *Raja Petra Raja Kamarudin v. Menteri Hal Ehwal Dalam Negeri* [2008] 1 LNS 920.

[58] *Raja Petra Raja Kamarudin v. Menteri Hal Ehwal Dalam Negeri* [2008] 1 LNS 920, 936.

[59] The preamble of the ISA stipulated: "An Act to provide for the internal security of Malaysia, preventive detention, the prevention of subversion, the suppression of organised violence against persons and property in specified areas of Malaysia, and for matters incidental thereto. [West Malaysia - 1st August. 1960; East Malaysia - 16th September. 1963.]

A reading of the express provisions of the ouster clause reveals that where any act is done or decision is made by the Minister when exercising his discretionary power in accordance with the ISA, then no judicial review is permissible. Judicial review is precluded or ousted where the Minister has acted, or exercised his discretion to make a decision, within the purview of the Act...They can only mean one thing namely that the Minister's decision is not completely unfettered and arbitrary but is confined by the provisions of the Act in question, here the ISA. The net result of according meaning to those words "in accordance with the Act" is that where the Minister has acted outside the purview of the express objects of the ISA, then he has acted outside the jurisdiction accorded to him by the Act. In short he has acted ultra vires the object of the Act. In such an instance the ouster clause does not come into play, or does not take effect. This result follows from a simple reading of the section 8B.[60]

Thus, the Court in essence held that due to the ouster clause inserted in the ISA, the courts in Malaysia were not authorised to challenge the discretionary power of the Minister to detain an individual as long as the grounds of detention was consistent with the objectives of the ISA. However, if the grounds for the detention were completely beyond the ambit of the ISA then the court's power to examine the validity of the detention order would not be ousted by section 8B of the ISA. To this end, the High Court provided examples of the circumstances which would warrant the judiciary to exercise its jurisdiction in safeguarding the liberty of the individual:

If for example, the Minister were to say that the grounds for the exercise of his discretion are that the colour of the detainee's hair is red and therefore this is the basis for invoking his powers under the ISA, then the immediate clear and simple response to the effect of s. 8B would be that the section would not in such a instance have the effect of ousting the jurisdiction of the Court in seeking to review the exercise of discretion. This is because the Minister in putting forward such grounds is clearly acting ultra vires his powers under the ISA. The Minister's powers under the ISA are circumscribed by the provision and object of the Act itself.[61]

However, it should be stressed here that the High Court also clarified that section 8B of the ISA only ousted the jurisdiction of the courts to examine detention orders passed under section 8. It did not apply to detention orders passed under section 73(1) of the ISA. In this context, reference can be made to the case of *Borhan Hj Daud & Ors v. Abd Malek Hussin.*[62] The respondent in this case was

---

WHEREAS action has been taken and further action is threatened by a substantial body of persons both inside and outside Malaysia - (1) to cause, and to cause a substantial number of citizens to fear, organized violence against persons and property; and (2) to procure the alteration, otherwise than by lawful means, of the lawful Government of Malaysia by law established; AND WHEREAS the action taken and threatened is prejudicial to the security of Malaysia; AND WHEREAS Parliament considers it necessary to stop or prevent that action.

Now therefore PURSUANT to Article 149 of the Constitution BE IT ENACTED by the Duli Yang Maha Mulia Seri Paduka Baginda Yang di-Pertuan Agong with the advice and consent of the Dewan Negara and Dewan Ra'ayat in Parliament assembled, and by the authority of the same."

[60] *Raja Petra Raja Kamarudin v. Menteri Hal Ehwal Dalam Negeri* [2008] 1 LNS 920, 937.

[61] Ibid.

[62] *Borhan Hj Daud & Ors v. Abd Malek Hussin* [2010] 8 CLJ 656.

detained under section 73(1) of the ISA and claimed that his detention for 57 days was unlawful. He further claimed that he was assaulted and tortured while he was in police custody. The High Court held that the detention of the respondent was a *mala fide* exercise of the power under the ISA.[63]

It is evident from the discussion of the above cases that the Malaysian Judiciary while examining the detention orders passed under the ISA shied away, in most cases, from undertaking an activist role for preventing the executive's attempt to arbitrarily encroach on the liberty of individuals. The deferential attitude of the judiciary can aptly be summarized in its own words:

our [courts] duties are not to substitute our decision for that of the executive. The courts are only concerned with the procedural aspects of the exercise of executive discretion. The courts have no interest, nor desire, to embark upon trespassing into the domains of the legislature or the executive.[64]

The judiciary's unwillingness to offer detainees an effective remedy in cases of arbitrary encroachment on their liberty created a sense that the Minister under the ISA could subject detainees to the most colorable exercise of the power of preventive detention with impunity.

4.3.1.1.5 Abuse of the Powers Concerning Preventive Detention Under the ISA

At the time drafting of the ISA, RH Hickling noted: "I could not imagine then, that the time would come when the power of preventive detention, carefully and deliberately interlocked with Article 149 of the Constitution, would be used against political opponents, welfare workers and others dedicated to nonviolent, peaceful activities."[65] However, in the absence of adequate safeguards circumscribing the scope of the exercise of the extraordinary power of preventive detention under the ISA, the government of the day used the power in an unrestrained manner, thus proving wrong the prediction of Hickling.

First, there were instances where the exercise of the power of preventive detention under the ISA could not properly be brought within the purview of the Act. For instance, in the case of *Tan Sri Raja Khalid Raja Harun v. the Inspector-General of Police*,[66] it was alleged that when the applicant served as a member of the loans committee of the Perwira Habib Bank, he provided consultancy services through his company, the Malayan Commercial Services Sdn Bhd, which in turn resulted in the loans committee approving large sums of money as loans to various parties, thereby

---

[63] Ibid.

[64] *Theresa Lim Chin Chin v. Inspector General of Police* [1988] 1 LNS 132.

[65] Hickling (2007), http://www.telegraph.co.uk/news/obituaries/1548788/Professor-Hugh-Hickling.html

[66] *Tan Sri Raja Khalid Raja Harun v. the Inspector-General of Police* [1987] CLJ (Rep) 1014.

causing the bank to suffer substantial losses. Subsequently, the applicant was detained under section 73(1) of the ISA on the basis that the police officer had.

> reason to ... believe that the substantial losses suffered by the bank caused by the manner in which loans were approved by the loans committee to certain parties, particularly through the acts of the applicant, has evoked feelings of anger, agitation, dissatisfaction and resentment among members of the armed forces and it is likely that such feelings may be ignited and lead to their resorting to violent action and thereby affect the security of the country.[67]

Contrary to the Police's claim, the above facts reveal that the alleged crimes of the appellant were neither subversive nor posed any threats to the security of Malaysia. Rather they were purely criminal in nature and, as such, the appellant could more properly have been dealt with under the ordinary criminal law framework.[68]

Second, there were numerous instances of abuse of the power of preventive detention under the ISA for detaining political opponents of the government of the day. For instance, just before the 1969 general election, practically the whole Labor Party leadership was detained under the ISA for its alleged links with the outlawed Malaysian Communist Party.[69] However, the Labor Party claimed that these detentions were carried out to "make it easier for the [Ruling] Alliance to win the polls".[70]

Moreover, on 27 October 1987, the Operation *Lalang* saw the detention of 106 individuals under the ISA. Most of the detainees were prominent opposition leaders, academics, prominent human rights activists, university lecturers, businessmen and so on. Although the government of Mahathir Mohamad alleged that these individuals were involved in activities "prejudicial to the security of Malaysia," a term often used as the basis of arrest and detention in Malaysia,[71] it is evident that the extraordinary power of preventive detention became an efficient tool for detaining the critics of the government. In this context, Kua Kia Soong—an advisor of the Malaysian Human Rights Organization, Suara Rakyat Malaysia (SUARAM)— opined that "Operation Lalang bore the mark of Dr. Mahathir's autocracy... – the rule of law... [was] flouted in such a cynical way that all his critics and dissidents across the Malaysian political spectrum were hauled in that dragnet".[72]

On 10 April 2001, Batu MP Chua Tian Chang, activist Hishamuddin Rais and Hulu Kelang assemblyman Saari bin Sungib were arrested under section 73(1) of the ISA.[73] Later, on 20 and 26 April 2001, Gobalakrishnan a/l Nagapan—a former MP—and Raja Petra Raja Kamarudin—the editor of Malaysia Today—were

---

[67] *Tan Sri Raja Khalid Raja Harun v. the Inspector-General of Police* [1987] CLJ (Rep) 1014, 1015.

[68] *Tan Sri Raja Khalid Raja Harun v. the Inspector-General of Police* [1987] CLJ (Rep) 1014, 1016.

[69] Ibid. Drummond and Hawkins (1970), p. 322.

[70] Drummond and Hawkins (1970), p. 322.

[71] See above n 6, pp. 240–241.

[72] Soong   (2016),   http://www.freemalaysiatoday.com/category/opinion/2016/11/23/ detention-without-trial-biggest-obstacle-to-transformation/

[73] Internal Security Act, 1960 (ISA) in sec. 73(1) provided: Any police officer may without warrant arrest and detain pending enquiries any person in respect of whom he has reason to believe—(a) that there are grounds which would justify his detention under section 8; and (b) that he has acted

arrested under the same provision of the ISA. Subsequently, the Home Minister issued preventive detention orders against them under Section 8 of the ISA[74] as they were allegedly "plotting the violent overthrow of the government of Dr. Mahathir Mohamad".[75] These individuals were released from preventive custody in June 2003. Upon release, they sued the Chief of Police, the Home Ministry and the government for unlawful detention under the ISA and for defamation.[76] The Court of Appeal in pronouncing a judgment 2 years after the ISA had been repealed in 2012 shed light on the flagrant abuse of the power of preventive detention under the ISA:

> the instant case involved not persons in criminal activities for personal gain, but persons in political activities whom the police stated it 'had reason to believe' was involved in activities prejudicial to the security of Malaysia but at the trial, neither evidence for such reason to believe was produced nor reasons for the failure to do so was presented in the trial, leading to the conclusion there was no basis for the arrest and detention, and that the plaintiffs were arrested for their political activities. The grounds of detention were frivolous and devoid of merit, the detainees were not a threat to the security and that they were detained for their political beliefs… Such… detention strikes at the very heart of a democracy, and in our view, is a much more serious assault on personal liberty and with very much less justification for arrest and detention. The Constitution expects of the police a fair, objective and independent approach in respect of political activities, as it is the key to a functioning democratic system.[77]

However, 5 years after his first detention, on September 12, 2008, Raja Petra was once again detained under the ISA for a period of 2 years. It was claimed that the reason behind his detention was his allegation that the then Deputy Prime Minister, Najib Tun Razak, and his wife were involved in the murder of a Mongolian woman.[78] Furthermore, Tan Hoon Cheng, a newspaper reporter was also detained on the same day for reporting a ruling party MP's racist statement that Chinese citizens of Malaysia were "squatters and therefore not entitled to rights".[79]

Third, there were also several instances where the reason behind the detention of individuals was their political belief or alleged subversive activities. The detainees were asked questions regarding their political activities rather than issues pertaining to national security during police investigation. For instance, in the case of *Mohamad*

---

or is about to act or is likely to act in any manner prejudicial to the security of Malaysia or any part thereof or to the maintenance of essential services therein or to the economic life thereof.

[74] Ibid. Sec. 8(1) provided that '[i]f the Minister is satisfied that the detention of any person is necessary with a view to preventing him from acting in any manner prejudicial to the security of Malaysia or any part thereof or to the maintenance of essential services therein or to the economic life thereof, he may make an order (hereinafter referred to as "a detention order") directing that that person be detained for any period not exceeding 2 years.'

[75] Sydney Morney Herald (2002), http://www.smh.com.au/articles/2002/03/29/1017206152563.html

[76] The Sun Daily (2014), http://www.thesundaily.my/news/1265144

[77] *Tan Sri Norian Mai & Ors v Chua Tian Chang & Ors* [2015] 4 MLJ 464, 485.

[78] Tyler and Brent (2013), pp. 549–550.

[79] Ibid.

Ezam Mohd Nor v. Ketua Polis Negara,[80] the appellant's affidavit claimed that he was questioned about his political stand and the reasons for his opposition to Mahathir and the *Barisan Nasional* (BN)—then the ruling coalition. The interrogation team had also asked him to abandon Anwar Ibrahim, who was sacked as the Deputy Prime Minister on 2 September 1998, and had subsequently cautioned him that he could only remain in the United Malays National Organisation (UMNO)—then the ruling party—provided he no longer raised issues concerning the alleged injustice perpetrated against Anwar.[81]

Finally, in the absence of a maximum period prescribed by the ISA for keeping an individual in preventive custody, the ISA, as discussed earlier in Sect. 4.3.1.1.3, was used by the government of the day for unduly depriving individuals of their liberty for a prolonged period of time. Such prolonged detention often led to torture and mistreatment of the detainees. For instance, Syed Husin Ali—then the President of Party Rakyat Malaysia—who was detained for 6 years, alleged that he was slapped, kicked, and pushed during his detention.[82] He also claimed that the Police questioned him for 11 hours each day for 2 weeks.[83]

The Inquiry Panel established by the SUHAKAM to investigate the abuses of the power of preventive detention under the ISA found that

> there appears to be sufficient evidence to justify a finding of cruel, inhume or degrading treatment of some of the detainees who testified before the Inquiry Panel. Slapping of detainees, forcible stripping of detainees for non medical purposes, intimidation, night interrogations and deprival of awareness of place and the passage of time, would certainly fall within the ambit of cruel, inhuman and degrading treatment.[84]

Thus, it is manifestly evident from the above discussion that the power of preventive detention under the ISA was used for extraneous purposes. The ISA was ultimately repealed on 22 June 2012 after nearly 52 years of operation.

4.3.2   The Security Offences (Special Measures) Act, 2012 (SOSMA)

The SOSMA was also enacted in pursuance of Article 149(1) of the Federal Constitution and came into force on 22 June 2012 to replace the ISA. Section 32 of the Act repeals the ISA.[85] However, such repeal did not affect the detention orders

---

[80] *Mohamad Ezam Mohd Nor v. Ketua Polis Negara* [2002] 4 CLJ 309.

[81] *Mohamad Ezam Mohd Nor v. Ketua Polis Negara* [2002] 4 CLJ 309, 329.

[82] See above n 6, p. 258.

[83] See above n 6, p. 258.

[84] See above n 35, part V.

[85] Security Offences (Special Measures) Act, 2012 (SOSMA) in sec. 32 states that 'The internal Security Act 1960 [*Act 82*] is repealed'.

which were previously issued under the ISA. Thus, those who were detained under the ISA continued to be interned.[86]

4.3.2.1 The Purpose and Scope of the SOSMA

The long title of the SOSMA states that it has been enacted "to provide for special matters relating to security offences for the purpose of maintaining public order and security for connected matters". The SOSMA in the same manner as the ISA, as pointed out earlier in Sect. 4.3.1.1.1, incorporates in its recital the first sentence of Article 149(1). Additionally, unlike the ISA, which included in its recital two paragraphs to Article 149(1), the SOSMA in its recital includes four paragraphs to Article 149(1), namely paragraphs (a), (b), (d) and (f). Thus, the recital of the SOSMA reads as follows:

> WHEREAS action has been taken and further action is threatened by a substantial body of persons both inside and outside Malaysia—.
>
> 1. to cause, or to cause a substantial number of citizens to fear, organized violence against persons or property;
> 2. to excite disaffection against the Yang di-Pertuan Agong;
> 3. which is prejudicial to public order in, or the security of, the Federation or any part thereof; or
> 4. to procure the alteration, otherwise than by lawful means, of anything by law established;
>
> AND WHEREAS Parliament considers it necessary to stop such action;

The SOSMA Bill tabled before the Parliament broadly defined "security offence", as used in the long title, as "an act prejudicial to national security and public safety".[87] The adoption of such a broad definition would have given the government significant leeway to categorize a wide range of situations, such as demonstrations to oppose unpopular actions, as being prejudicial to the national security.[88] For instance, the government could decide that the popular "clean elections" campaign run by *Bersih*—an electoral reform group—to compel the government to change the electoral practices at the time when the SOSMA Bill was tabled before the Parliament, posed a threat to the "national security and public safety".[89]

However, when the SOSMA came into effect in June 2012, the term "security offences" got an even wider meaning. Section 3 contained in Part I stipulates that "security offences" for the purposes of the SOSMA are "the offences specified in the First Schedule" of the Act, which are the offences listed in Chapters VI and VIA

---

[86] Malaysiakini (2013), http://freemalaysiakini2.blogspot.com/2013/07/suhakam-sosma-could-violate-human-rights.html

[87] Suara Rakyat Malaysia (SUARAM) (2014), p. 4, http://www.suaram.net/wordpress/wp-content/uploads/2014/12/Suaram-Human-Rights-Overview_2014_9-Dec.pdf

[88] Spiegel (2012), http://www.hrw.org/sites/default/files/related_material/2012_Malaysia_EastWest.pdf

[89] Ibid.

of the Penal Code. Chapter VI of the Penal Code deals with "Offences against the State,"[90] while Chapter VIA deals with the "Offences relating to Terrorism".[91]

It is pertinent to note here that within 2 years of coming into force of the SOSMA, it was amended by the Security Offences (Special Measures) (Amendment) Act, 2014.[92] The Amendment Act further broadened the definition of the term "security offences" by adding the following to the offences that had already been specified in the First Schedule of the SOSMA: (a) the offences listed in Chapter VIB of the Penal Code, which deals with "Organised Crimes"; and (b) Part IIIA of the Anti-Trafficking in Persons and Anti-Smuggling of Migrants Act, 2007.

It should be stressed here that offences relating to smuggling of migrants as stipulated by the Anti-Trafficking in Persons and Anti-Smuggling of Migrants Act, 2007 are not the kind of offences which the Reid Commission envisaged could be brought within the purview of any law passed in pursuance of Article 149 of the Constitution, which, as discussed earlier in Sect. 2.6.3, is contained in Part XI of the Constitution titled "Special Powers Against Subversion, Organised Violence and Acts and Crimes Prejudicial to the Public and Emergency Powers".

However, notwithstanding the substantial broadening of the scope of the definition of "security offences" in 2014, the Parliament on 15 June 2015 passed yet another amendment to further widen the scope of the definition. Following this latest amendment, the term "security offences", as used in Section 3 of Part I of the SOSMA, also includes the acts criminalized by the Special Measures Against Terrorism in Foreign Countries, 2015.[93]

Thus, in light of the extensive amendments, it is evident that the "security offences" for the purposes of the SOSMA are those offences specified in abovementioned chapters of the Penal Code, Part IIIA of the Anti-Trafficking in Persons and Anti-Smuggling of Migrants Act, 2007 and the Special Measures Against Terrorism in Foreign Countries, 2015. Consequently, when a person has committed one of those offences, he will be tried in accordance with the procedure laid down in the SOSMA by virtue of section 2 and the First Schedule to the SOSMA.

---

[90] "Offences against the State" include waging or attempting to wage war against the Yang di-Pertuan Agong, Rulers or Yang di-Pertuan Negeri ("the Rulers"), hurting the Rulers, deposing the Rulers, overthrowing by criminal force the government of Malaysia or of any of the states and assaulting Members of Parliament or State Legislative Assemblymen in their exercise of their duties.

[91] The specific terrorist offences provided for in the Penal Code from Sections 130C to 130 T include committing terrorist acts, providing explosives, recruiting persons to join terrorist groups, providing training or facilities to terrorists, giving of support, directing terrorist activities and criminal conspiracy.

[92] Security Offences (Special Measures) (Amendment) Act, 2014. The Act came into force on 31 December 2014.

[93] The Special Measures Against Terrorism in Foreign Countries, 2015 has been enacted to enable the executive to deal with "persons who engage in the commission or support of terrorist acts involving listed terrorist organizations in a foreign country or any part of a foreign country and for related matters".

It is also noteworthy that in addition to the Security Offences (Special Measures) (Amendment) Act, 2014 discussed above, major amendments were also introduced to the Penal Code and Criminal Procedure Code in order to render their provisions consistent with the SOSMA.

An attempt will now be made to examine the provisions of the SOSMA concerning preventive detention.

4.3.2.2 The Provisions Concerning Preventive Detention Under the SOSMA

Part II, titled "Special Powers for Security Offences", of the SOSMA contains provisions empowering police officers to exercise the special power of preventive detention. Subsection 1 of Section 4 read together with subsection 4 authorizes the detention of an individual on the suspicion of him being involved in "security offences" for an initial period of 24 hours. Furthermore, section 4(5) empowers "a police officer of or above the rank of Superintendent of Police" to extend the detention from a period of 24 hours to 28 days.[94]

However, section 4(11) of the SOSMA provides that section 4(5), which empowers the Police to extend the period of preventive detention of an individual, "shall be reviewed every 5 year and shall cease to have effect, unless upon review a resolution is passed by both Houses of Parliament to extend the period of operation" of that provision. It should be stressed here that the provision contained in section 4(5) was supposed to lapse on 31 July 2017.[95] However, the Parliament chose to extend the operation of the provision for another 5 years notwithstanding concerns raised by international non-governmental organizations, such as the Human Rights Watch.[96]

It is evident from the above discussion that the SOSMA brought within its purview a wide range of offences, which are already criminalized under the ordinary criminal law framework, as grounds warranting the exercise of the power of preventive detention to detain suspected individuals. Thus, the SOSMA concentrates too much power in the executive to take away the liberty of individuals. An attempt will now be made to examine the safeguards afforded by the SOSMA to mitigate the harshness of the exercise of the power of preventive detention.

---

[94] Ibid. In Sec. 4(5) states that 'a police officer of or above the rank of Superintendent of Police may extend the period of detention for a period of not more than 28 days, for the purpose of investigation'.

[95] Human Rights Watch (2017), https://www.hrw.org/news/2017/03/30/malaysia-reject-security-bill-extension

[96] Ibid.

4.3.2.2.1   The Safeguards Afforded to Detainees Under the SOSMA

(a) Prohibition on Detention due to One's Political Belief

The SOSMA in section 4(3) states that "no person shall be … detained solely for his political belief or political activity". The terms "political belief" and "political activity" have, subsequently, been defined in section 4(12) of the Act to mean "engaging in lawful activity through-(a) the expression of an opinion or the pursuit of a course of action made according to the tenets of a political party that is at the relevant time registered under the Societies Act, 1966 as evidenced by (i) membership of or contribution to that party; or (ii) open and active participation in the affairs of that party; (b) the expression of an opinion directed towards any Government in the Federation; or (c) the pursuit of a course of action directed towards any Government in the Federation".

It seems that this safeguard was inserted in the SOSMA to obviate the possibility of abuse of the power concerning preventive detention for political purposes, which, as pointed earlier in Sect. 4.3.1.1, was a common phenomenon during the lifetime of the ISA. However, this safeguard stipulated by Section 4(3) of the SOSMA, as will be demonstrated in the forthcoming discussion in Sect. 4.3.2.3, has no practical application for preventing the use of the power of preventive detention for political persecution.

(b) Right to be Informed of the Grounds of Detention

In accordance with Articles 5 and 151(1)(a) of the Malaysian Constitution, Section 4(2) of the SOSMA obligates the police officer detaining an individual to inform the detainee of the grounds of detention "as soon as may be". However, the utility of this safeguard is greatly undermined due to the fact that the timeframe for communicating the grounds of detention to a detainee has been kept indeterminate. This argument is bolstered by the fact that 11 of the 146 individuals who were kept in preventive custody under the SOSMA until November 2014 were not informed of the grounds of their detention.[97]

(c) Right to Communicate with the Family Members

Although the Constitution of Malaysia does not impose any obligation on detaining authorities to provide an individual detained under a preventive detention law access to their family members, section 5(1)(a) of the SOSMA makes this right available to the detainee immediately after his detention. It should be stressed here that this right afforded by the SOSMA is an important guarantee against detention incommunicado. However, practice shows that the police in some instances have denied detainees the right to be given immediate access to their family members in clear violation of the express guarantee contained in section 5(1)(a) of the SOSMA.[98]

---

[97] See above n 87.

[98] Ibid.

(d) **Right to Consultation with a Legal Practitioner**

Section 5(1)(b) of the SOSMA also gives a detainee the right to consult a legal practitioner of his choice. However, this safeguard is qualified by the terms of subsection (2) of the same provision. For Section 5(2) of the SOSMA provides a police officer of or above the rank of a Superintendent of Police the discretion to deny a detainee the right to consult a lawyer for 48 hours if he is of the view-

> (a) there are reasonable grounds for believing that the exercise of this right will interfere with the evidence connected to the security offence; (b) it will lead to harm to another; (c) it will lead to alerting of other person who is a suspect for the commission of such an offence but not yet arrested; (d) it will hinder the recovery of property obtained through the commission of such an offence.

It should be stressed here that the police have also shown a reluctance to extend the above safeguard to detainees. For instance, in violation of the provisions of section 5(1) and (2) of the SOSMA, 11 individuals kept in preventive custody under the SOSMA until November 2014 were deprived of the right to consult a lawyer for as many as 8 days.[99]

In light of the above discussion, it is evident that the SOSMA affords limited safeguards to detainees. For instance, the SOSMA has not incorporated the safeguard contained in Article 151(1)(b) of the Federal Constitution, which, as discussed earlier in Sect. 2.6.3(c), guarantees an individual detained under a preventive detention law the right to have his detention order reviewed before a quasi-judicial board. It is further evident that the limited guarantees afforded to detainees under the SOSMA have frequently been flouted by the detaining authority. It should be stressed here that the guarantee of limited of safeguards and their subsequent flouting are at odds with the pledges made by Najib Razak—the then Prime Minister—in the Parliament on 15 September 2011—only 9 months before the coming into force of the SOSMA. As the Prime Minister told the Parliament:

> Basically, …[this law] will be aimed at maintaining peace and wellbeing. Above all, the government will ensure that the rights of those involved will be safeguarded. Legislation formulated will take into consideration fundamental rights and freedom based on the Federal Constitution.[100]

---

[99] Ibid.

[100] The Star Online (2011), http://www.thestar.com.my/story/?file=%2F2011%2F9%2F15%2Fnati on%2F20110915205714

4.3.2.3 Abuse of the Powers Concerning Preventive Detention Under the SOSMA

Although the ISA, as pointed out earlier in Sect. 4.3.1.1.2, was repealed in 2012,[101] Malaysians were not allowed to breathe a sigh of relief for long due to the enactment of yet another preventive detention law, i.e. the SOSMA, which raised legitimate fears that the government would rely on it to oppress its critics. These fears were realized when three political detentions occurred under the SOSMA within a few years of its enactment.[102]

First, Khairuddin Abu Hassan, former Vice-Head of the Batu Kawan division of the former ruling party—UMNO—was originally detained by the Malaysian police on 23 September 2015 under the SOSMA on the suspicion of seeking to topple the government and was subsequently charged under: a) section 124 L of the Penal Code for "attempting to sabotage the state", and b) section 124 K of the Penal Code for "sabotage".[103] Second, Hassan's lawyer, Matthias Chang, was paradoxically also detained under the SOSMA after he visited Hassan at the Dang Wangi Police Station in Kuala Lumpur on 8 October 2015 and similar charges were brought against him.[104] According to the Amnesty International, the detentions of Hassan and Chang were aimed at preventing their submission of reports, which apparently contained "evidence of money-laundering involving Prime Minister Najib Razak, in connection with the state-owned investment company 1Malaysia Development Berhad (1MDB)", to the US Federal Bureau of Investigation (FBI).[105] Thus, it is evident that the preventive detention powers under the SOSMA were used in this instance "as part of a concerted effort to silence those exposing corruption in relation to the 1MDB".[106] Consequently, the High Court held that the charges brought against Hassan and Chang did not fall within the purview of the SOSMA.[107]

Third, Maria Chin Abdullah, the Chairman of pro-democracy group, *Bersih*, was detained for an initial period of 24 hours under the SOSMA on 18 November 2016—a day before the demonstration organized by *Bersih* demanding the resignation of Prime Minister Razak over his alleged involvement in the 1MDB scandal,

---

[101] Security Offences (Special Measures) Act, 2012 (SOSMA) in sec. 32 states that 'The internal Security Act 1960 [Act 82] is repealed'.

[102] Ibid. In Sec. 4(5) empowers a police officer of or above the rank of Superintendent of police to extend the 24 h of detention to not more than 28 days without trial for the purpose of investigation.

[103] Amnesty International (2015), https://www.amnesty.org/download/Documents/ASA2824892015ENGLISH.pdf

[104] Zolkepli (2015), http://www.thestar.com.my/news/nation/2015/10/08/matthias-chang-detained-under-sosma/

[105] Ibid. Prime Minister Razak had faced criticism since the Wall Street Journal reported in 2015 that around US$700m from state fund, 1Malaysia Development Berhad (1MDB), was diverted into his personal bank account. Wright and Clark, (2015), https://www.wsj.com/articles/SB10130211234592774869404581083700187014570

[106] Ibid.

[107] The Sun Daily (2015), http://www.thesundaily.my/news/1614590

took place.[108] The Inspector-General of Police claimed that in the raid conducted at the *Bersih* Office on 18 November, documents were found which showed that Abdullah had committed an offence under Section 124C[109] of the Penal Code by threatening the practice of parliamentary democracy in Malaysia. On 20 November 2016, 2 days after Abdullah's initial detention, her lawyer—Eric Paulsen—confirmed to the media that her detention under the SOSMA had been extended to another 28 days.[110] Since the SOSMA is an Act which is aimed at providing for special measures relating to security offences and in section 4(3) specifically states that "[n]o person shall be arrested and detained … solely for his political belief or political activity," it is evident that the government once again misused the power of preventive detention—in this instance for silencing a 60-year-old civil society leader just before the peaceful *Bersih* rally.

Finally, it is pertinent to note here that the SOSMA has also been used as an instrument for torturing detainees. For instance, on 29 October 2019, 12 individuals were detained under the SOSMA on suspicion of being associated with the Liberation Tigers of Tamil Eelam (LTTE).[111] The Police not only extended their initial detention for a further period of 28 days in pursuance of section 4(5) of the SOSMA but 5 of these detainees also claimed that the police tortured and mistreated them in preventive custody to extract false confessions.[112]

4.3.3 The Prevention of Crime Act, 1959 (PCA)

On 2 October 2013, the Parliament passed the Prevention of Crime (Amendment and Extension) Act, which came into effect on 2 April 2014, for amending and extending the operation of the Prevention of Crime Act, 1959. The long title of the original Act of 1959 stated that it was enacted to provide for "the more effectual prevention of crime in Peninsular Malaysia and for the control of criminals, members of secret societies and other undesirable persons, and for matters incidental thereto". However, the Amendment Act amended the long title by substituting the word "Peninsular'" with "throughout". Thus, the PCA now has effect throughout Malaysia.

---

[108] The Guardian (2016), https://www.theguardian.com/world/2016/nov/19/thousands-call-for-malaysian-prime-minister-najib-razak-to-quit

[109] The Malaysian Penal Code in sec. 124C stipulates that '[w]hoever attempts to commit an activity detrimental to parliamentary democracy or does any act preparatory thereto shall be punished with imprisonment for a term which may extend to 15 years.'

[110] Zurairi (2016), http://www.themalaymailonline.com/malaysia/article/lawyer-maria-chin-to-be-held-full-28-days-under-sosma#l4WzKEhEcH54Bmdd.97

[111] Singh(2020),https://www.nst.com.my/news/crime-courts/2020/02/567658/ag-drops-charges-against-12-accused-supporting-ltte

[112] See above n 87, p. 7.

The Prevention of Crime (Amendment) Act, 2015 further amended the long title of the PCA by inserting the words "secret societies" after the word "terrorists". Therefore, according to the amended long title, the PCA will now be relied on for not only preventing crime throughout Malaysia but also for controlling terrorists.

Furthermore, although the PCA was originally an ordinary criminal legislation, the recent amendments transformed it into a security legislation through the insertion of a recital in pursuance of Article 149(1) of the Federal Constitution. An attempt will now be made to discuss the provisions of the POTA concerning: a) the arrest of an individual prior to subjecting him to preventive detention; and b) preventive detention.

4.3.3.1 The Provisions Concerning Arrest Under the PCA

Section 3(1) of the PCA authorises a police officer to arrest any individual without the precondition of a warrant "if he has reason to believe that grounds exist which would justify the holding of an inquiry into the case of that person under" the Act. Following arrest, the PCA obligates the police to produce the arrested individual before a Magistrate within 24 hours[113] and also requires the case to be referred to the Public Prosecutor for direction within 7 days.[114]

Subsequently, the Magistrate can remand the arrested individual in police custody for a period of 21 days provided a police officer not below the rank of an Inspector produces a written statement stating that there are grounds for believing that the individual concerned is a member of any of the eight types of criminal organizations, termed "registrable categories", listed in the First Schedule to the PCA.[115] Before the expiry of 21 days, the Magistrate can issue another order for remanding the arrested individual for a further period of 38 days upon the receipt of two statements:

(i) "a statement in writing signed by the Public Prosecutor stating that in his opinion sufficient evidence exists to justify the holding of an inquiry" by an Inquiry Officer; and.

(ii) "a statement in writing signed by a police officer not below the rank of an Inspector stating that it is intended to hold an inquiry into the case of that person".[116]

It is, therefore, evident that even before any inquiry is conducted to determine whether there are valid reasons to keep an individual in custody, he can be detained for a period of 59 days—initially for a period of 21 days and subsequently for an additional 38 days—by the orders of a Magistrate. As to the inquiry mentioned

---

[113] PCA Section 3(2).

[114] Ibid., Sec. 3(1a).

[115] Ibid., Sec. 4(1); First Schedule to PCA.

[116] Ibid., Sec. 4(2).

above, it is striking that the PCA does not specify the procedure that needs to be followed by an Inquiry Officer for determining whether there are valid reasons for keeping the arrested individual in custody. Rather it merely stipulates that the inquiry is to be held "in such manner" and "in accordance with [such] procedure" as directed by the Prevention of Crime Board, which is appointed by the YDPA.[117] Furthermore, the PCA does not stipulate any timeframe within which the Inquiry Officer should submit its report for the consideration of the Board.

It is striking that the Inquiry Officer—whose report forms the basis for the Board's decision to detain an individual under section 19A(1)—is also appointed by the executive in pursuance of section 8 of the PCA. Consequently, it can be argued that the executive would be able to exert undue influence on the Officer, which in turn would impede the latter's competence to conduct a fair and impartial inquiry.

4.3.3.2 The Provisions Concerning Preventive Detention Under the PCA

The Amendment Act of 2014 inserted a new Part IVA, titled "Detention Orders", in the PCA. The provisions contained in Part IVA permit preventive detention of individuals, who are suspected of being members of any of the "registrable categories" listed in the First Schedule to the PCA. In this context, it should be stressed here that these "registrable categories" include triads, human trafficking groups, drug trafficking organizations, and terrorist organizations. Section 19A(1) of the PCA, which empowers a Prevention of Crime Board constituted under section 7B to detain a person after considering the report of the Inquiry Officers, provides:

> The Board may, after considering the report of the Inquiry Officer… direct that any registered person be detained under a detention order for a period not exceeding two years, and may renew any such detention order for a further period not exceeding two years at a time, if it is satisfied that such detention is necessary in the interest of public order, public security or prevention of crime.

Thus, it is evident from a perusal of the above provision that the PCA authorises the exercise of the power of preventive detention to detain suspected members of criminal organisations discussed above if such detention is considered necessary "in the interest of public order, public security or preventive of crime". Furthermore, the PCA empowers a Board to keep an individual in preventive custody for an indefinite period of time as there is no limit as to the number of times a detention order can be extended.

4.3.3.3 The Constitution of a Prevention of Crime Board

The PCA, as amended in 2014, stated that the Prevention of Crime Board constituted under section 7B would comprise of a Chairman and four other members appointed by the YDPA—the head of state. Furthermore, the Act, as amended in

---

[117] Ibid.

2014, also stipulated the qualification of the Chairman of the Board by stating in section 7B(1)(a) that he "shall be or have been, or be qualified to be, a judge of the Federal Court, the Court of Appeal or a High Court". But the Prevention of Crime (Amendment) Act, 2015 not only amended the constitution of the Board under the PCA but also altered the qualification required to be the Chairman of the Board. According to the amended section 7B(1) of the PCA, the Board shall comprise of a Chairman, a Deputy Chairman and "not less than 3 and not more than six other members". Thus, the membership of the Board has significantly been increased. Furthermore, the amended 7B(1)(a) of the PCA removes the necessity for the Chairman of the Board to: a) be a sitting judge; or b) be a retired judge; or c) have the qualifications to become a judge. Rather it stipulates that any legally qualified person with 15 years "experience in the legal field" can be appointed as a Chairman of the Board. However, the PCA, as amended in 2014 and 2015, does not prescribe the qualifications of the Deputy Chairman and the other members of the Board. Furthermore, the members of the Board do not enjoy any security of tenure. For section 7B(4) of the PCA provides the head of the state the unconstrained power to revoke the appointment of any member of the Board at his pleasure. Thus, the PCA gives the executive branch of the government the unfettered discretion to pack the Board with loyalists and to subsequently remove them at its whim. Consequently, the Board can hardly be expected to be independent of the wishes of the executive when deciding whether there are valid reasons for detaining an individual under the PCA. These issues are further compounded by the fact that the government shrouds the identity of the members of the Board under a thick veil of secrecy. For instance, when the Home Minister was asked in 2014 about the identity of the members of the Board, he merely stated that "they… [are] individuals of high integrity with more than 27 years of experience in the field of security. They are also law practitioners of good credentials".[118]

4.3.3.4   The Safeguards Stipulated by the PCA

In light of the discussion in the preceding sections, it is evident that the PCA, as amended extensively in 2014 and 2015, has given the executive branch significant leeway to arbitrarily deprive individuals of their liberty. However, the PCA does afford certain safeguards to detainees. An attempt will now be made to evaluate the adequacy of these safeguards.

(a) **Right not to be Detained for One's Political Belief or Political Activity**
    In the same manner as the SOSMA, the PCA, as amended in 2015, prohibits in section 4(2A) the detention of an individual on account of his pollical belief or activity. It is pertinent to note here that as of December 2019, 908 individuals have been kept in preventive custody under the PCA.[119] However, when ques-

---

[118] See above n 87, p. 5.

[119] See above n 87, p. 6.

tioned about the types of crimes those who had been detained under the PCA in the year 2014 were suspected of committing, the Home Minister refused to disclose any information on the plea that such disclosure would interfere with the police investigation. Such non-disclosure has the impact of defeating the very objective of inserting the safeguard contained in section 4(2A). For it allows the executive to conceal any information about the detention of its political adversaries.

(b) **Right to be informed of the Grounds of Detention and Right to Make a Representation against the Advisory Board**

The Federal Constitution, as discussed earlier in Sect. 2.6.3(c), in Article 151 provides an individual detained under a preventive detention law the right to be informed of the grounds of detention and the right to make a representation before an Advisory Board. The PCA originally did not contain any provision guaranteeing these safeguards. However, following the amendment of 2015, the PCA in section 19A(4) now stipulates that:

A copy of every detention order made by the Board under subsection (1) shall as soon as may be after the making of the order be served on the person to whom it relates, and every such person shall be entitled to make representations to an Advisory Board constituted under Clause (2) of Article 151 of the Federal Constitution in accordance with the prescribed procedures.

It is striking from a perusal of the above provision that the PCA only requires the detaining authority to serve the detention order on an individual kept in preventive custody. It does not, however, obligate the detaining authority to ensure that the order contains the actual grounds of detention. It is further striking that the PCA does not specify a timeframe for serving the order to the detainee. Therefore, it can be argued that the absence of these guarantees impedes the detainee's right to make an effective representation against his detention.

(c) **Right to Judicial Review**

The PCA in section 19A(2) of the PCA gives a detainee the right to challenge the decision of the Prevention of Crime Board which ordered its detention. As it stipulates: "The direction of the Board under subsection (1) shall be subject to review by the High Court." However, it seems that such a review would be limited to examining whether the detention is in compliance with the procedural requirements prescribed by the PCA. For like section 8B of the ISA, which specifically ousted the jurisdiction of the courts to examine the legality of detention orders, the PCA also contains a similar ouster clause in section 15A(1), which stipulates that:

There shall be no judicial review in any court of, and no court shall have or exercise any jurisdiction in respect of, any act done or decision made by the Board in the exercise of its discretionary power in accordance with this Act, except in regard to any question on compliance with any procedural requirement in this Act governing such act or decision.

Furthermore, the PCA defines "judicial review" in identical terms as section 8C of the ISA. For section 15A(2) of the PCA provides that:

"judicial review" includes proceeding instituted by way of—

(a) an application for any of the prerogative orders of mandamus, prohibition and certiorari;
(b) an application for a declaration or an injunction;
(c) a writ of habeas corpus; and
(d) any other suit, action or other legal proceedings relating to or arising out of any act done or decision made by the Board…

In light of the above provisions and of the past culture of judicial deference, it can be argued that the judiciary will refuse to scrutinize detention orders issued in pursuance section 19A(2) of the PCA unless the facts revealed non-compliance with the procedural requirements in the Act.

It is evident from the above discussion that the PCA authorises detaining authorities to keep an individual in preventive custody for an indefinite period of time. Furthermore, the PCA does not provide a detainee access to lawyers or family members. The absence of such express guarantees, as discussed earlier in Sect. 3.2, gives rise to the objectionable possibility of torture and mistreatment of detainees. Furthermore, the judiciary will be tempted to maintain its previous tradition, as discussed above in Sect. 4.3.1.1.4(b), of holding that denial, for instance, of access to a lawyer will not vitiate a preventive detention order issued under the PCA by *mala fide*.

It is noteworthy that during Malaysia's second Universal Periodic Review (UPR) at the 25th session of the United Nations Human Rights Council in Geneva, Switzerland, on 25 October 2013, the Council recommended, among other things, that both the SOSMA and the PCA should be amended in order to ensure Malaysia's compliance with its international human rights obligations. However, notwithstanding such a recommendation, no changes have so far been introduced to either the SOSMA or PCA for affording improved safeguards to detainees.

4.3.4 The Prevention of Terrorism Act, 2015 (POTA)

Following the Parliament's unanimous approval of the White Paper, titled "Towards Combating the Threat of Islamic State", on 26 November 2014, the Government expressed its commitment to enact the POTA for effectively dealing with the threat identified in the White Paper.[120] Najib Razak—the then Prime Minister—in a speech before the Parliament underscored the necessity for the adoption of stern legal measures for combating terrorism.[121] He was particularly concerned about those Malaysians who had returned home after fighting beside Islamic State (IS) militants in Syria and Iraq, as they could potentially instil their radical ideology into the minds of others.[122] Razak also noted that 39 Malaysians were at the time fighting in

---

[120] Singh(2015),http://www.todayonline.com/world/asia/new-law-gives-malaysia-teeth-fight-against-terror

[121] Zeldin (2014) http://www.loc.gov/lawweb/servlet/lloc_news?disp3_l205404242_text

[122] Ibid.

Syria, while another 40 (including foreign nationals) were arrested in 2014 for alleged terrorism-related offences.[123] During the debate on the POTA, Ahmad Zahid Hamidi—the then Home Minister—in line with previous assertions of the Prime Minister stated that the threat of terrorism was real which required preventive measures.[124] Thus, it is evident that the enactment of the POTA, according to the regime, was considered a necessity for dealing with the perceived threat of terrorism posed by Malaysians sympathetic towards the IS.[125] However, neither the Prime Minister nor the Home Minister articulated why the perceived threat of terrorism could not adequately be addressed by the existing security laws, such as the SOSMA and PCA, which also authorize the exercise of the extraordinary power of preventive detention.

Accordingly, the International Commission of Jurists (ICJ) expressed its concern about the imminent enactment of the POTA in an open letter addressed to the speaker of the Lower House of the Malaysian Parliament (Yang di-Pertua Dewan Rakyat), on 6 April 2015, in the following words:

> The Malaysian government has not demonstrated how the current security situation in Malaysia meets the very high threshold required for the creation of a system of administrative security detention. The government has also not demonstrated why the existing criminal law, law enforcement, and criminal justice system, properly resourced and implemented, cannot adequately address acts of terrorism.[126]

It seems that in order to dispel any doubt about the necessity of enacting the POTA, reports of the Malaysian Police detaining 17 people suspected of plotting to carry out terror attacks in Kuala Lumpur conveniently surfaced on the eve of the parliamentary vote on the law.[127] Consequently, the POTA was passed by the Parliament with unprecedented haste, which reflected a sense of desperation on the part of the ruling coalition. The deliberations on the POTA Bill spanned for nearly 15 hours and the Bill was ultimately enacted into law at 2:26 am in the morning of 7 April 2015.[128] The POTA came into effect on 1 September 2015.

---

[123] Ibid.

[124] The Khilafah (2015), http://www.khilafah.com/malaysias-prevention-of-terrorism-act-2015-another-step-that-pleases-america/

[125] Tisdall (2015), https://www.theguardian.com/world/2015/apr/07/malaysia-najib-razak-terrorism-threat-human-rights-detention-without-trial

[126] Zarifi (2015), http://icj2.wpengine.com/wp-content/uploads/2015/04/Malaysia-Open-Letter-to-Parliament-on-POTA-Advocacy-open-letter-2015-ENG.pdf

[127] TheGuardian (2015), https://www.theguardian.com/world/2015/apr/06/malaysia-arrests-17-for-alleged-terrorist-attack-plot-in-kuala-lumpur

[128] Malaysian Insider (2015) https://sg.news.yahoo.com/parliament-passes-controversial-anti-terrorism-law-79-60-225022379.html

4.3.4.1   Procedures for Arrest and Preventive Detention Under the POTA

Before the passing of the POTA, the Prevention of Crime Act, 1959 (PCA), as discussed earlier in Sect. 4.3.3, was extensively amended and extended for more effective prevention of crime and terrorism in Malaysia.[129] The Prevention of Crime
(Amendment and Extension) Act 2014 amending the PCA was passed by the
Parliament on 2 October 2013 and it came into effect on 2 April 2014. Thus, within
a year of the coming into force of the PCA, the Government felt the necessity of
passing yet another Act, the POTA, to deal with terrorism. The long title of the POTA
reads as follows.

> An Act to provide for the prevention of the commission or support of terrorist acts involving
> listed terrorist organizations in a foreign country or any part of a foreign country and for the
> control of persons engaged in such acts and for related matters.

An attempt will now be made to examine the procedural provisions concerning
arrest and preventive detention under the POTA.

4.3.4.1.1   Interpretation of the Relevant Words Used in the POTA

According to Diane Webber, terrorism is the "[u]nlawful use, or threat, of violence
by non-state actors, against persons, property, critical infrastructures, or key
resources, intended to intimidate or coerce a government, or all or part of the general public, in furtherance of political, religious or ideological objectives".[130]
Subsequently, Webber correctly warns about the risk of adopting a broader definition of terrorism. For, doing so provides significant leeway to the executive branch
of government to preventively detain terror suspects for offences that lie outside the
purview of terrorist activities.[131]

Notwithstanding the above cautionary words, section 2 of the POTA, titled
"Interpretation", does not attempt to interpret or define many of the words used in
the text of the act, including "terrorism", "terrorist" and "terrorist acts". This is
indeed paradoxical considering the POTA has been enacted for preventing terrorism-
related offences.

Furthermore, rather than defining the phrase "terrorist act", which is used several
times throughout the POTA, section 2 states that the words "terrorist act" has the
same meaning assigned to it by the Penal Code. The Penal Code defines a terrorist
act in section 130B(2), Chapter VIA:

> ....as an act or threat of action within or beyond Malaysia where

---

[129] The Prevention of Crime (Amendment) Act, 2015 amended the long title of the Prevention of
Crime Act and states that it is enacted to provide for "the more effectual prevention of crime
throughout Malaysia and for the control of criminals, members of secret societies, terrorists and
other undesirable persons, and for matters incidental thereto".

[130] Webber (2016), p. 5.

[131] Ibid., p. 6.

(a) the act or threat falls within subsection (3)[132] and does not fall within subsection (4)[133];
(b) the act is done or the threat is made with the intention of advancing a political, religious or ideological cause; and
(c) the act or threat is intended or may reasonably be regarded as being intended to—(i) intimidate the public or a section of the public; or (ii) influence or compel the Government of Malaysia or the Government of any State in Malaysia, any other government, or any international organization to do or refrain from doing any act.

The wordings of section 130B(2)(b) of the Penal Code are particularly troubling as this subsection does not clarify whether its scope extends to include any protests or strikes carried out with the intention of expressing political views different to that of the government of the day. Moreover, section 130B(3)(j) of the Code states that an act prejudicing "national security or public safety" will amount to a "terrorist act". This section, however, does not specify the actions which would prejudice "national security or public safety".

In the same vein, the words "engagement in the commission or support of a terrorist act" as used in section 4(1)(a) of the POTA have not specifically been explained anywhere in the Act. Rather what constitutes such engagement has been left at the discretion of a police officer. Section 4 also uses the words "listed terrorist organizations in a foreign country or any part of a foreign country" and for the interpretation of "listed terrorist organizations" reference should be made to another Statute as section 2 of the POTA states that "listed terrorist organization" means any specified entity declared under sections 66B[134] and 66C[135] of the Anti-Money Laundering,

---

[132] The Penal Code in s 130B(3) provides that 'An act or threat of action falls within this subsection if it—(a) involves serious bodily injury to a person; (b) endangers a person's life; (c) causes a person's death; (d) creates a serious risk to the health or the safety of the public or a section of the public; (e) involves serious damage to property; (f) involves the use of firearms, explosives or other lethal devices; (g) involves releasing into the environment or any part of the environment or distributing or exposing the public or a section of the public to—(i) any dangerous, hazardous, radioactive or harmful substance; (ii) any toxic chemical; or (iii) any microbial or other biological agent or toxin; (h) is designed or intended to disrupt or seriously interfere with, any computer systems or the provision of any services directly related to communications infrastructure, banking or financial services, utilities, transportation or other essential infrastructure; (i)is designed or intended to disrupt, or seriously interfere with, the provision of essential emergency services such as police, civil defence or medical services; (j)involves prejudice to national security or public safety; (k) involves any combination of any of the acts specified in paragraphs (a) to (j), and includes any act or omission constituting an offence under the Aviation Offences Act 1984 [Act 307]'.

[133] The Penal Code in s 130B(4) provides that 'An act or threat of action falls within this subsection if it—(a) is advocacy, protest, dissent or industrial action; and (b) is not intended—(i) to cause serious bodily injury to a person; (ii) to endanger the life of a person; (iii) to cause a person's death; or (iv) to create a serious risk to the health or safety of the public or a section of the public'.

[134] The Anti-Money Laundering, Anti- Terrorism Financing and Proceeds of Unlawful Activities Act of 2001 in sec. 66B(1) provides that "where the minister of home affairs is satisfied on information given to him by a police officer that—(a) an entity has knowingly committed, attempted to commit, participated in committing or facilitated the commission of, a terrorist act; or (b) an entity is knowingly acting on behalf of, at the direction of, or in association with, an entity referred to in paragraph (a),the minister of home affairs may, by order published in the Gazette, declare the entity to be a specified entity".

[135] Ibid. In sec. 66C(1) provides that "Where the Security Council of the United Nations decides, in pursuance of Article 41 of the Charter of the United Nations, on the measures to be employed to

Anti- Terrorism Financing and Proceeds of Unlawful Activities Act of 2001. Furthermore, section 13(1) uses imprecise words, such as engagement "in the interest of the security of Malaysia or any part of Malaysia" and "in the interest of the security of Malaysia", as grounds for satisfying the executive to detain suspected terrorists.

Thus, it is evident that the provisions of the POTA are drafted in a very broad and ambiguous manner, which in turn provides considerable leeway to the detaining authority to rely on the power of preventive detention for extraneous purposes to impose arbitrary restrictions on the liberty of individuals. In this context, the cautionary words of Kofi Annan, the former Secretary General of the United Nations, regarding the response of states to terrorism are noteworthy:

> Our responses to terrorism, as well as our efforts to thwart it and prevent it, should uphold the human rights that terrorists aim to destroy. Respect for human rights, fundamental freedoms and the rule of law are essential tools in the effort to combat terrorism – not to be sacrificed at a time of tension.[136]

4.3.4.1.2 Procedure Prior to the Bringing of an Arrested Person Before a Magistrate

Section 3(1) of the POTA, in the same manner as the PCA, empowers any police officer to detain a person without any warrant on reasonable belief that there are grounds which would justify that person being made subject to an inquiry. The case of such a detained person is required to be brought before the Public Prosecutor within 7 days of his arrest[137] and the detained person must be brought before the Magistrate within 24 hours of his arrest.[138]

(a) **Production of an Arrested Person before the Magistrate**

After the arrested person is produced before the Magistrate, section 4(1)(a) of the POTA, like the PCA, requires the production of a statement in writing signed by a police officer not below the rank of an inspector stating that

---

give effect to any of its decisions and calls upon the Government of Malaysia to apply those measures, the Minister of Home Affairs may, by order published in the Gazette, make such provision as may appear to him to be necessary or expedient to enable those measures to be effectively applied.(2) Where an order under subsection (1) makes provision to the effect that there are reasonable grounds to believe that an entity designated by the Security Council of the United Nations is engaged in terrorist acts, the order under subsection (1) shall be deemed, with effect from the date of the order, to be an order declaring that entity to be a specified entity under subsection 66B(1);.

[136] Moon (2003), http://www.un.org/sg/STATEMENTS/index.asp?nid=275

[137] Prevention of Terrorism Act 2015 (POTA), sec 3(2) ('When a person is arrested… the case shall be referred by the police officer to the Public Prosecutor for direction not later than 7 days from the date of arrest').

[138] Ibid. In Sec. 3(3) ("Any person arrested… shall, unless sooner released, be taken without unreasonable delay, and in any case within 24 h (excluding the time of any necessary journey) before a Magistrate").

there are grounds for believing that the name of the person who is engaged in the commission or support of terrorist acts involving listed terrorist organizations in a foreign country or any part of a foreign country should be entered in the Register.

Consequently, the Magistrate shall remand the person in police custody for a period of 21 days and in the absence of such a statement and grounds the arrested person shall be released. If the person so remanded in police custody is not released sooner, then in pursuance of section 4(2) he shall before the expiry of the remand period be again brought before the Magistrate. The Magistrate is authorized to further remand the person for 38 days upon the receipt of two statements in writing— one signed by the Public Prosecutor stating that in his opinion sufficient evidence exists to justify the holding of an inquiry by an Inquiry Officer, who will be required to inquire and report on whether there exists reasonable grounds for holding the belief that the detainee "is engaged in the commission or support of terrorist activities listed terrorist organizations in a foreign country or any part of a foreign country"[139] and the other by a police officer not below the rank of an Assistant Superintendent stating that there indeed exists an intention to hold such an inquiry into the case of the detainee.[140]

It is striking that in the same manner as the PCA, the POTA also permits the detention of a person for a period of 59 (21 + 38) days even before an inquiry into the reasonableness of continuing his detention. Furthermore, during this period, the detainee has not been afforded essential safeguards, such as communication with family members or a legal practitioner of his choice, for mitigating the harshness of

---

[139] POTA, sec. 4(2)(a)(i) read together with s 10(1). Section 4(2)(a)(i) provides that "Any person remanded… shall, unless sooner released, on or before the expiry of the period for which he is remanded, be taken before a Magistrate, who shall—

(a) on production of—

(i) a statement in writing signed by the Public Prosecutor stating that in his opinion sufficient evidence exists to justify the holding of an inquiry under section 10;

…

order the person to be remanded in custody for a period of 38 days;"

Section 10(1) states that "[w]hen any person is brought before an Inquiry Officer… the Inquiry Officer shall inquire and report in writing to the Board whether there are reasonable grounds for believing that the person is engaged in the commission or support of terrorist acts involving listed terrorist organizations in a foreign country or any part of a foreign country".

[140] POTA, sec. 4(2)(a)(ii) read with s 10(1). Section 4(2)(a)(ii) stipulates that 2) Any person remanded under paragraph (1)(a) shall, unless sooner released, on or before the expiry of the period for which he is remanded, be taken before a Magistrate, who shall—

1. (a) on production of—

…

(i) a statement in writing signed by a police officer not below the rank of Assistant Superintendent stating that it is intended to hold an inquiry into the case of that person under section 10,

order the person to be remanded in custody for a period of 38 days;"

his detention order. Consequently, it can be argued that this leaves the door wide open for the executive branch of government to detain its political adversaries at its whim for almost 2 months.

(b) Inquiry Conducted by an Inquiry Officer

Although the POTA, as pointed out above, provides for an inquiry into the reasonableness of continuing the detention of an individual by an Inquiry Officer, it does not shed light on the procedure to be followed at such an inquiry.[141] Rather, like the PCA, the POTA leaves it to the discretion of a Prevention of Terrorism Board—the members of which are to be appointed by the YDPA—to determine the manner in which the inquiry should be conducted and to prescribe the procedure to be followed at such an enquiry. Since an inquiry into the necessity of continuing the detention of an individual has a significant impact on one of his most important liberties, namely the right to liberty, it can strongly be argued that sufficient specificity with respect to the process of gathering and subsequent reviewing of necessary information would have ensured the objectivity of the inquiry.

Furthermore, although the government has constantly claimed that the new security laws will not be used to detain any person for his political belief, the POTA in pursuance of the provisions of section 9 entrusts the Minister of Home Affairs with the power to appoint the officer who will hold an inquiry into the necessity of continuing the detention of an individual under the POTA.[142] It can hardly be expected from an officer appointed by the regime to conduct an objective inquiry and to subsequently submit an unbiased report in pursuance of section 12 within such period as may be prescribed by the Minister by regulations made under the POTA. Although, unlike the repealed ISA,[143] the POTA does not empower the Minister of Home Affairs to order the detention of a person, it is evident that the Minister still has a substantial involvement in some of the important procedures under the POTA, which can have adverse consequences for the liberty of the detained individual. If the Minister prescribes by regulation an unduly long period of time for the submission of the inquiry report, there is no scope for raising any question and the arrested person will continue to be detained even before the Prevention of Terrorism Board has, as will be discussed below, the opportunity to order a preventive detention order against him.

---

[141] POTA, Sec. 10(2).

[142] POTA, Sec. 9(2) (providing that a police officer cannot be appointed as an inquiry officer).

[143] ISA in section 8(1) stipulated that 'If the Minister is satisfied that the detention of any person is necessary with a view to preventing him from acting in any manner prejudicial to the security of Malaysia or any part thereof or to the maintenance of essential services therein or to the economic life thereof, he may make an order (hereinafter referred to as a detention order) directing that that person be detained for any period not exceeding 2 years'.

4.3.4.2 Constitution of the Prevention of Terrorism Board

Unlike the repealed ISA, which as pointed out above, empowered the Minister of Home Affairs to order the preventive detention of an individual, the power to detain a person under the POTA is entrusted with the Prevention of Terrorism Board.[144] Section 8(1) of the POTA spells out the composition of the Prevention of Terrorism Board. The Board is to be composed of: "(a) a Chairman, who shall be a legally qualified person with at least 15 years experience in the legal field; (b) a Deputy Chairman; and (c) not less than three and not more than six other members". Furthermore, these members are to be appointed by the YDPA.

It is evident that the POTA does not require the Chairman of the Board to be a past or present Judge of the superior courts or to be even qualified to hold judicial office. Rather it merely requires the Chairman to be someone who has had legal experience. This paves the way for the executive to appoint as Chairman a lawyer who it believes shares the same political ideology. It is also striking that the POTA is silent as to the qualifications of other members of the Board. The failure to specifically stipulate the qualifications of the members makes the whole process of issuance of the detention order by the Board susceptible to abuse. For the executive can pack the board with government loyalists, who in turn can unduly influence the proceedings of the Board according to the designs of the government at the expense of the liberty of an individual kept in preventive custody. Furthermore, although members of the Board are to remain in office for a period not exceeding 3 years, the YDPA has been empowered by section 8(4) of the POTA to revoke at his whim the appointment of any member of the Board at any time. The absence of security of tenure has the impact of further impeding the ability of the Board to act independently of the influences of the designs of the government.

4.3.4.3 Preventive Detention by the Order of the Board

The Prevention of Terrorism Board if after considering two sets of reports—one a complete report of an investigation conducted by a police officer into the arrested person[145] and the other from the Inquiry Officer[146]—

---

[144] POTA, sec. 13(1) (providing that "(1) Whenever the Board, after considering—

(a) the complete report of the investigation submitted under subsection 3(4); and
(b) the report of the Inquiry Officer submitted under section 12,

is satisfied with respect to any person that such person has been or is engaged in the commission or support of terrorist acts involving listed terrorist organizations in a foreign country or any part of a foreign country, the Board may, if it is satisfied that it is necessary in the interest of the security of Malaysia or any part of Malaysia that such person be detained, by order ("detention order") direct that such person be detained for a period not exceeding 2 years.

[145] This report is required to be submitted under section 3(4) of the POTA.
[146] The report of the Inquiry Office must be submitted to the Board in pursuance of section 12(1) of the POTA.

is satisfied with respect to any person that such person has been or is engaged in the commission or support of terrorist acts involving listed terrorist organizations in a foreign country or any part of a foreign country, the Board may, if it is satisfied that it is necessary in the interest of the security of Malaysia or any part of Malaysia that such person be detained, by order ("detention order") direct that such person be detained for a period not exceeding two years.[147]

In the same manner as detention orders under the PCA[148] and the repealed ISA,[149] a detention order under the POTA can further be extended by the Board under section 17 for a period of 2 years at a time. Furthermore, section 17(5) imposes no restriction on the number of times the period of detention may be extended by the Board under the POTA. Thus, the extraordinary power of indefinite preventive detention has been brought back under the disguise of new labels almost 3 years after the ISA was repealed.

4.3.4.4 The Safeguards Provided to the Detainee Under the POTA

It has been discussed earlier in Sect. 2.6.3 that the Federal Constitution in Articles 5 and 151 provide certain fundamental rights and safeguards which in the absence of any specific exclusion clause in the Constitution should be read into the POTA and should be available to any person detained under the security laws passed in accordance with the Constitution. An attempt will now be made to analyze the adequacy of the safeguards provided to individuals detained in pursuance of the POTA.

(a) **Prohibition on Arrest and Detention Solely on Account of One's Political Belief**

Section 4 of the POTA, titled "Procedure before Magistrate", in subsection (3) states that "[n]o person shall be arrested and detained under this section solely for his political belief or political activity". Furthermore, sub-section (6) of the same section provides that

For the purpose of this section, "political belief or political activity" means engaging in a lawful activity through—

---

[147] POTA, sec. 13(1).

[148] The PCA in section 19A(1) provides that 'The Board may, after considering the report of the Inquiry Officer submitted under section 10 and the outcome of any review under section 11, direct that any registered person be detained under a detention order for a period not exceeding 2 years, and may renew any such detention order for a further period not exceeding 2 years at a time, if it is satisfied that such detention is necessary in the interest of public order, public security or prevention of crime'.

[149] The ISA in sec. 8(7) empowered the Minister to extend the duration of a preventive detention order for a period not exceeding 2 years at a time either on the same grounds on which the original order was made or on different grounds or partially on the same and partially on different grounds.

(*a*) the expression of an opinion or the pursuit of a course of action made according to the tenets of a political party that is at the relevant time registered under the societies Act 1966 [*Act 335*] as evidenced by—

(i) membership of or contribution to that party; or
(ii) open and active participation in the affairs of that party;

(*b*) the expression of an opinion directed towards any government in Malaysia; or

(*c*) the pursuit of a course of action directed towards any government in Malaysia.

It seems that the above provisions contained in section 4(3) and (6) are simply reproduced from the similar provisions provided for by section 4(3) and (12) of the SOSMA.[150] However, the arrests and detentions, as pointed out earlier in Sect. 4.3.2.3, of Datuk Seri Khairuddin Abu Hassan and Maria Chin Abdullah under the SOSMA for voicing their opposition to the then Prime Minister's handling of the 1MDB's finances demonstrate that the presence of the provision in section 4(3) is inadequate for safeguarding against political detention and as such is merely ornamental in nature. In this context, the observations of SUARAM in the "Malaysia Human Rights Report 2015" is noteworthy:

> The detention of Khairuddin Abu Bakar and Matthias Chang in 2015 marked the first political detentions under SOSMA. It exposed the government's justification of preventing "security offences" through introducing this Act.[151]

Furthermore, the Malaysian Bar Council in a Press Release on the POTA on 5 April 2015 stated that.

> [t]he exclusion of 'political belief and political activity' as a ground for detention under POTA is… false comfort… We also note that in the past, politicians and political activists had been detained under the ISA for activities that were nonetheless viewed as prejudicial to national security or public order.[152]

Therefore, it can be argued that the government's use of the SOSMA for political purposes in contravention of the guarantee contained in section 4(3) of the same gives rise to the concern that the similar guarantee contained in the POTA will also prove ineffective for preventing political detentions.

---

[150] SOSMA in section 4(3) states that 'no person shall be arrested and detained solely for his political belief or political activity' and in s 4(12) provides that "engaging in lawful activity through-(a) the expression of an opinion or the pursuit of a course of action made according to the tenets of a political party that is at the relevant time registered under the Societies Act, 1966 as evidenced by (i) membership of or contribution to that party; or (ii) open and active participation in the affairs of that party; (b) the expression of an opinion directed towards any Government in the Federation; or (c) the pursuit of a course of action directed towards any Government in the Federation."

[151] Suaram (2015), http://www.suaram.net/wordpress/wp-content/uploads/2017/02/HR2015.pdf

[152] Thiru (2015), Available at http://www.malaysianbar.org.my/press_statements/press_release_%7C_prevention_of_terrorism_bill_2015_violates_malaysias_domestic_and_international_commitments_is_an_affront_to_the_rule_of_law_and_is_abhorrent_to_natural_justice.html

(b) **Right to Representation before An Advisory Board**

In order to ensure the facilitation of an effective representation against the detention order, it is imperative that the detainee is provided the grounds of detention in precise terms.[153] To this end the POTA in section 13(9), which is a verbatim reproduction of section 19A(4) of the PCA, merely stipulates that

A copy of every detention order made by the Board under subsection (1) shall as soon as may be after the making of the order be served on the person to whom it relates, and every such person shall be entitled to make representations to an Advisory Board constituted under Clause (2) of Article 151 of the Federal Constitution in accordance with the prescribed procedures.

It is evident from the above provision that the POTA only imposes an obligation on the detaining authority to serve the detention order on the detainee without simultaneously specifying that such an order should contain the actual grounds of the detention. This is a deviation from the practice followed in other polities. For it is a common practice for preventive detention laws to specifically stipulate that the grounds of detention should be communicated to the detainee so as to assist him in making an effective representation against the detention order.[154] Furthermore, this provision of the POTA has kept the timeframe for serving the detention order on the detainee unspecified through the use of the ambiguous expression "as soon as may be". It can, therefore, be strongly argued that this provision vests wide discretion in the detaining authority to withhold the grounds of the detention, which renders the detainee's right to make a representation against the detention order a meaningless exercise.

(c) **Representation by a Legal Practitioner**

The POTA in section 10(6) takes away from the detainee at the inquiry stage one of the essential guarantees, namely the right to consult and to be defended by a legal practitioner, provided for by Article 5 of the Federal Constitution, in the following words:

---

[153] Bari (2017), p. 50.

[154] For instance, the Special Powers Act, 1974, which is the permanent prevention detention legislation in Bangladesh, in sec. 8(2) provides that: "In the case of a detention order, the authority making the order shall inform the person detained under that order of the grounds of his detention at the time he is detained or as soon thereafter as is practicable, but not later than 15 days from the date of detention".

In India, the National Security Act, 1980, in sec. 8(1) states that: "When a person is detained in pursuance of a detention order, the authority, making the order shall as soon as may be, but ordinarily not later than 5 days and in exceptional circumstances and for reasons to be recorded in writing, not later than 10 days from the date of detention, communicate to him the ground on which the order has been made and shall afford him the earliest opportunity of making representation against the order to the appropriate Government."

In Pakistan, the Security of Pakistan Act, 1952, in sec. 6(2) requires the detaining authority to inform the individual kept in preventive custody "the grounds of his detention at the time he is detained or as soon thereafter as is practicable, but not later than 15 days from the date of detention".

Neither the person who is the subject of the inquiry nor a witness at an inquiry shall be represented by an advocate and solicitor at the inquiry except when his own evidence is being taken and recorded by the Inquiry Officer.

Furthermore, section 13, titled "Power to Order Detention and Restriction", also does not specify the right of the detainee to be represented by a legal practitioner before the Board. The failure to afford the detainee the right to be represented before the Board by a lawyer further weakens the safeguard provided for by section 13(9) and renders it impossible for the detainee to mount an effective and meaningful representation against the detention order.

(d) **Access to Judicial Review**

Section 13 of the POTA, which deals with the issuance of the detention order by the Board, in subsection (10) states that "[t]he direction of the Board... shall be subject to review by the High Court". However, following in the footsteps of the PCA, such review under the POTA is also limited to examining a detention order's compliance with the procedural requirements in the Act. As section 19(1), titled "Detention and Restriction Orders", seeks to exclude judicial review of acts and decisions of the Prevention of Terrorism Board on substantive grounds in the following terms:

There shall be no judicial review in any court of, and no court shall have or exercise any jurisdiction in respect of, any act done or decision made by the Board in the exercise of its discretionary power in accordance with this Act, except in regard to any question on compliance with any procedural requirement in this Act governing such act or decision.

The meaning of "judicial review" is subsequently articulated in Section 19(2) of the POTA and includes any proceeding instituted by way of "a writ of *habeas corpus*". Thus, it is evident that although the POTA in section 13(10) makes the direction or decision of the Prevention of Terrorism Board subject to review by the High Court, section 19(1) ousts the jurisdiction of any court to examine the detention orders on their merit.

It might be recalled from the discussion in Sect. 2.6.3 that the proviso to Article 149(1) of the Federal Constitution of Malaysia permits preventive detention laws, among other things, to be inconsistent with the guarantees afforded by Article 5, which includes the right to challenge the legality of one's detention order before the High Court. Thus, the ouster of the authority of the judiciary to examine the legality of a detention order under the POTA is warranted by the supreme law of the nation,[155] depriving in the process a detainee of an efficacious remedy in case of an insidious encroachment on liberty and leaving his fate at the mercy of the detaining authority.

---

[155] The Federal Constitution of Malaysia, 1957 Art. 4(1)—providing that the "Constitution is the supreme law of the Federation".

4.4   Comparing and Contrasting the Preventive Detention Provisions of the SOSMA, PCA, and POTA with the ISA

The ISA, as pointed out earlier in Sect. 4.3.1.1, in its almost 52 years of operation, had been used as an instrument for suppressing the political adversaries of the government of the day. Having critically examined the provisions concerning preventive detention under the SOSMA, PCA and POTA, an attempt will now be made to compare these with those of the ISA.

4.4.1   Use of Vague Terms and of Offences Criminalized Under the Ordinary Criminal Law as Grounds for Preventive Detention

Like the ISA, both the PCA and the POTA use vague words as grounds for exercising the power of preventive detention. The PCA employs in section 19A(1) words, such as "in the interest of public order, public security or prevention of crime", for satisfying the Prevention of Crime Board that it is necessary to detain individuals. In the same vein, the POTA uses in section 13(1) vague words, such as engagement "in the commission or support of terrorist acts" and "in the interest of the security of Malaysia", as sufficient grounds for depriving individuals of their liberty. Furthermore, the POTA, as discussed earlier in Sect. 4.3.4.1, does not define the words "terrorism", "terrorist" and "terrorist acts". However, unlike the ISA, the SOSMA and PCA have also significantly broadened the scope of the power of preventive detention by incorporating, among other things, offences relating to smuggling of migrants, human trafficking, and drug trafficking, which are already criminalized under the ordinary criminal law framework and, consequently, are not recognized by Article 149(1) of the Constitution as grounds for permitting the enactment of preventive detention laws, as the basis for exercising the power of preventive detention.

4.4.2   The Body Entrusted with the Power to Exercise Preventive Detention

In the same manner as section 73(1) of the ISA, which authorized a police officer to exercise the power of preventive detention, the SOSMA in section 4 also empowers a police officer to preventively detain individuals. By way of contrast, the PCA and POTA authorize the Prevention of Crime Board and the Prevention of Terrorism Board respectively to order the detention of individuals in the interests of public order and public security. Thus, both these statutes leave the liberty of an individual at the broad discretion of a Board, which cannot be said to function independently of the influence of the executive as its members, as had been pointed out in Sects. 4.3.3 and 4.3.4, are not only appointed by the executive but they have also not been given security of tenure. Consequently, it can be argued that the vesting of extraordinary powers concerning preventive detention on a non-judicial body through the use of ambiguous terms increases the likelihood of the kind of abuse, which Malaysia had witnessed from 1960 to 2012 under the ISA occurring again. Furthermore, given the Malaysian judiciary's historical reluctance, as pointed out above in Sect. 4.3.1.1., in scrutinizing prevention detention orders, it is unlikely that it will thwart arbitrary encroachment on the liberty of individual under the PCA and POTA.

4.4.3   Maximum Period of Preventive Detention

Under both the PCA and POTA, as discussed earlier in Sects. 4.3.3 and 4.3.4, an arrested person, in the first place, can be remanded for a total period of 59 days—initially for 21 days and subsequently for a further 38 days on the order of the Magistrate pending an inquiry into the necessity of continuing the detention. Second, both the Acts are also silent as to the specific timeframe within which an arrested person is to be brought before an inquiry officer. Third, neither of these statutes stipulate the timeframe within which the inquiry officers should submit their report to the Boards. Thus, even before the Boards are given the opportunity to order an individual to be kept in preventive custody, the detainee can be deprived of his liberty. Furthermore, the Prevention of Crime Act Board and the Prevention of Terrorism Board, as pointed out earlier in Sects. 4.3.3 and 4.3.4, are empowered to issue orders directing an individual to be preventively detained for a period not exceeding 2 years, which is again subject to extension "for such further period not exceeding 2 years" at a time. Thus, it is evident that following in the footsteps of the ISA, both the PCA and the POTA also permit preventive detention for an indefinite period of time.

However, in light of the above discussion, it can strongly be argued that in comparison to the old ISA provisions, the provisions of the PCA and the POTA are more draconian in nature as they allow detention for a prolonged period even before formal preventive detention orders are issued by the respective Prevention Boards. The incorporation of such draconian provisions in the PCA and POTA, which permit indefinite detention of individuals, in turn has the disturbing impact of facilitating the violation of the fundamental human rights of individuals, such as the right not to be subjected to torture, cruel and degrading treatment—a right from which no derogation is permitted under any circumstances.[156] As the United Nations (UN) Special Rapporteur on torture noted: "the greater the uncertainty regarding the length of

---

[156] The human rights norms developed in the 1950s and 1960s, which find expression in the European Convention for the Protection of Human Rights and Fundamental Freedoms (ECHR) 1950 in article 3, the International Covenant on Civil and Political Rights (ICCPR) 1966 in article

time, the greater the risk of serious mental pain and suffering to the inmate that may constitute cruel, inhuman or degrading treatment or punishment or even torture".[157] Furthermore, the report concerning the Belmarsh Case, which was published in October 2004 by "11 consultant psychiatrists and one consultant clinical psychology",[158] revealed that the indefinite detention of individuals in the Belmarsh Prison caused "serious damage to the health of eight of the detainees".[159]

4.4.4 Access to Judicial Review

Following in the footsteps of section 8B of the ISA, section 15A(1) of the PCA and section 19(1) of the POTA also exclude the court's jurisdiction to review the legality of detention orders except on procedural grounds. It is, indeed, disturbing that Malaysia in the present era of human rights and constitutionalism has chosen to deprive detainees under the PCA and the POTA an important constitutional safeguard which is pivotal for preventing the unlawful deprivation of one the most fundamental rights, namely, the right to personal liberty. In this context, the observations of Justice Bhagwati in *Sampath Kumar v. Union of India*[160] regarding the importance of judicial review are noteworthy:

> judicial review is a basic and essential feature of the Constitution and no law passed by Parliament in exercise of its constituent power can abrogate it or take it away. If the power of judicial review is abrogated or taken away the Constitution will cease to be what it is. It is a fundamental principle of our constitutional scheme that every organ of the State, every authority under the Constitution, derives its power from the Constitution and has to act within the limits of such power... it is the judiciary which has to ensure that the law is observed and there is compliance with the requirements of law on the part of the executive and other authorities... the power of judicial review... is a most potent weapon in the hands of the judiciary for maintenance of the Rule of law. The power of judicial review is an integral part of our constitutional system and without it, there will be no Government of laws and the Rule of Law would become a teasing illusion and a promise of unreality.[161]

It is evident from the above discussion that both the PCA and POTA have not only brought back the wide powers concerning preventive detention as had been contained in section 8 of the ISA but also in some cases the provisions contained in the PCA and POTA are far more draconian than those of the ISA. In the absence of proper safeguards for preventing the arbitrary encroachment on the liberty of

---

26, and the American Convention on Human Rights (ACHR) 1969 in article 5, recognize the right not to be subjected to torture, cruel and degrading treatment as a non-derogable right.

[157] United Nations High Commissioner for Human Rights (2013), http://newsarchive.ohchr.org/en/NewsEvents/Pages/DisplayNews.aspx?NewsID=13859&LangID=E

[158] See above n 153, p. 53.

[159] Amnesty International UK (2004), www.amnesty.org.uk/press-releases/uk-lords-ruling-three-years-too-late-internees; Zayas (2005), p. 19.

[160] *Sampath Kumar v. Union of India* [1987] SC 386.

[161] *Sampath Kumar v. Union of India* [1987] SC 386, 388.

individuals, these statutes provide the executive the necessary ammunition to stifle legitimate political dissent. The broad scope of the powers under the PCA and POTA can be further gathered from a recent comment of the Malaysian Inspector General of Police to the effect that the enactment of these Acts has made the ISA "irrelevant".[162]

Accordingly, an attempt will be made in the next chapter, i.e., the Concluding Chapter, to put forward concrete recommendations for ensuring the maintenance of an appropriate balance between safeguarding national security and simultaneously observing respect for an individual's right to protection from arbitrary deprivation of liberty.

References

Amnesty International. (2015). *Urgent action. Free politician held for exposing corruption.* Available at https://www.amnesty.org/download/Documents/ASA2824892015ENGLISH.pdf

Amnesty International UK. (2004). *Press release: UK lords ruling: Three years too late for internees.* Available at www.amnesty.org.uk/press-releases/uk-lords-ruling-three-years-too-late-internees. Accessed 10 Dec 2013.

Bari, M. E. (2017). Preventive detention laws in Bangladesh and their increased use during emergencies: A proposal for reform. *Oxford University Commonwealth Law Journal., 17*(1), 45–46.

Basu, D. D., & Nandi, A. K. (2000). *Administrative law.* Kolkata: Kamal Law House.

Cook, H. (1992). Preventive detention – International standards and the protection of the individual. In S. Frankowski & D. Shelton (Eds.), *Preventive detention: A comparative and international law perspectives* (p. 25). New York: Springer.

Drummond, S., & Hawkins, D. (1970). The Malaysian Elections of 1969: An analysis of the campaign and the results. *Asian Survey, 10*(4), 320–322.

Final Report of Federation of Malaya Constitutional Commission (Reid Commission). (1957). *Submitted on 21 February 1957.*

Hector, C. (2006). *Detention without Trial Laws in Malaysia.* Available at http://www.malaysian-bar.org.my/human_rights/detention_without_trial_laws_in_malaysia_.html

Hickling, H. R. (1962). The first five years of the Federation of Malaya Constitution. *Malaya Law Review, 4,* 183.

Human Rights Commission of Malaysia. (2003). *Review of the Internal Security Act, 1960.* Available at http://www.suhakam.org.my/wp-content/uploads/2013/12/review-of-the-ISA-1960.pdf

Human Rights Watch. (2017). *Malaysia: Reject Security Bill Extension – Let Abusive Detention Provision Lapse.* Available at https://www.hrw.org/news/2017/03/30/malaysia-reject-security-bill-extension

Ki-Moon, B. (2003). *Secretary-General's statement at the Special Meeting of the Counter-Terrorism Committee with Regional Organizations.* Available at http://www.un.org/sg/STATEMENTS/index.asp?nid=275

Kumar, K. (2016). *IGP: New security laws "better than ISA".* Available at http://www.themalaymailonline.com/malaysia/article/igp-new-security-laws-better-than-isa

Malaysiakini. (2013). *Suhakam: SOSMA could violate human rights.* Available at http://freemalaysiakini2.blogspot.com/2013/07/suhakam-sosma-could-violate-human-rights.html

---

[162] Kumar (2016), http://www.themalaymailonline.com/malaysia/article/igp-new-security-laws-better-than-isa

Office of the United Nations High Commissioner for Human Rights. (2013). *Statement of the United Nations special Rapporteur on torture at the expert meeting on the situation of detainees held at the U.S. Naval Base at Guantanamo Bay.* Available at http://newsarchive.ohchr.org/en/NewsEvents/Pages/DisplayNews.aspx?NewsID=13859&LangID=E

Singh, B. (2015). *New law gives Malaysia teeth in fight against terror.* Available at http://www.todayonline.com/world/asia/new-law-gives-malaysia-teeth-fight-against-terror

Singh, S. (2020). *AG drops charges against 12 accused of supporting LTTE.* Available at https://www.nst.com.my/news/crime-courts/2020/02/567658/ag-drops-charges-against-12-accused-supporting-ltte

Soong Kua, K. (2016). *Detention without trial biggest obstacle to transformation.* Available at http://www.freemalaysiatoday.com/category/opinion/2016/11/23/detention-without-trial-biggest-obstacle-to-transformation/

Spiegel, M. (2012). Smoke and mirrors: Malaysia's "new" internal security act. *Asia Pacific Bulletin.* East West Centre: Washington, number 167. Available at http://www.hrw.org/sites/default/files/related_material/2012_Malaysia_EastWest.pdf

Suara Rakyat Malaysia (Suaram). (2014). *Malaysia: Human Rights Report Overview.* Available at http://www.suaram.net/wordpress/wp-content/uploads/2014/12/Suaram-Human-Rights-Overview_2014_9-Dec.pdf

Suaram. (2015). *Malaysia Human Rights Report VII.* Available At http://www.suaram.net/wordpress/wp-content/uploads/2017/02/HR2015.pdf

Sydney Morney Herald. (2002). *Royal revolutionary pays price for backing Anwar.* Available at http://www.smh.com.au/articles/2002/03/29/1017206152563.html

The Guardian. (2015). *Malaysia arrests 17 for alleged terrorist attack plot in Kuala Lumpur.* Available at https://www.theguardian.com/world/2015/apr/06/malaysia-arrests-17-for-alleged-terrorist-attack-plot-in-kuala-lumpur

The Guardian. (2016). *Thousands Call for Malaysian Prime Minister Najib Razak to Quit.* Available at https://www.theguardian.com/world/2016/nov/19/thousands-call-for-malaysian-prime-minister-najib-razak-to-quit

The Khilafah. (2015). *Malaysia's Prevention of Terrorism Act 2015: Another step that pleases America.* Available at http://www.khilafah.com/malaysias-prevention-of-terrorism-act-2015-another-step-that-pleases-america/

The Malaysian Insider. (2015). *Parliament passes controversial anti-terrorism law by 79 to 60 votes.* Available at https://sg.news.yahoo.com/parliament-passes-controversial-anti-terrorism-law-79-60-225022379.html

The Star Online. (2011). *PM Announces Repeal of ISA, Three Emergency Proclamation.* Available at http://www.thestar.com.my/story/?file=%2F2011%2F9%2F15%2Fnation%2F20110915205714

The Sun Daily. (2014) *Appeals court awards RM4.55m to Tian Chua, Hishamuddin Rais, 3 others.* Available at http://www.thesundaily.my/news/1265144

The Sun Daily. (2015) *Court rules charge against Khairuddin, chang does not fall under SOSMA.* Available at http://www.thesundaily.my/news/1614590

The Telegraph. (2007). *Professor hugh hickling.* Available at http://www.telegraph.co.uk/news/obituaries/1548788/Professor-Hugh-Hickling.html

Thiru Steven. (2015). *Press release: Prevention of Terrorism Bill 2015 violates Malaysia's domestic and international commitments, is an affront to the rule of law and is abhorrent to natural justice.*

Tisdall, S. (2015). *Malaysia uses specious terrorism threat to regress on human rights.* Available at https://www.theguardian.com/world/2015/apr/07/malaysia-najib-razak-terrorism-threat-human-rights-detention-without-trial

Tyler, J., & Brent, J. (2013). Preventive detention in Malaysia: Constitutional and judicial obstacles to reform and suggestions for the future. *Georgia Journal of International and Comparative Law, 41*(535), 549–550.

Webber, D. (2016). *Preventive detention of terror suspects: A new legal framework.* Routledge.

Wright, T., & Clark, S. (2015). *Investigators believe money flowed to Malaysian leader Najib's accounts Amid 1MDB Probe"*. Available at https://www.wsj.com/articles/SB10130211234592774869404581083700187014570

Yatim, R. (1995). *Freedom under executive power in Malaysia: A study of executive supremacy.* Kuala Lumpur: Endowment Publications.

Zarifi, S. (2015). *Open letter to parliament on POTA.* Available at http://icj2.wpengine.com/wp-content/uploads/2015/04/Malaysia-Open-Letter-to-Parliament-on-POTA-Advocacy-open-letter-2015-ENG.pdf

Zayas Alfred de. (2005). Human rights and indefinite detention. *International Review of the Red Cross, 87*(15), 19.

Zeldin, W. (2014). *Malaysia: Anti-terrorism law proposed.* Available at http://www.loc.gov/lawweb/servlet/lloc_news?disp3_l205404242_text

Zolkepli, F. (2015). *Matthias Chang detained under SOSMA.* Available at http://www.thestar.com.my/news/nation/2015/10/08/matthias-chang-detained-under-sosma/

Zurairi, A. R. (2016). *Lawyer: Maria Chin to be held for 28 days under SOSMA.* Available at http://www.themalaymailonline.com/malaysia/article/lawyer-maria-chin-to-be-held-full-28-days-under-sosma#l4WzKEhEcH54Bmdd.97

Chapter 5
Conclusion and Recommendations

Abstract The objective of this Chapter, in the first place, is to summarize the key arguments of this Book with a view to highlighting the weaknesses of the Malaysian Constitution's provisions, which give carte blanche power to the Parliament to enact laws conferring on the executive wide powers concerning the exercise of the power of preventive detention. Subsequently, in light of the standard constitutional model concerning preventive detention developed in Chap. 3 of this book, this Chapter will endeavour to put forward concrete recommendations for insertion of adequate safeguards in the Malaysian Constitution with a view to diminishing the possibility of abuse of the powers concerning preventive detention.

5.1 Introduction

An endeavour will be made in this Chapter to summarise the key arguments set out in the preceding four chapters with a view to highlighting the weaknesses of the Malaysian Constitution's provisions concerning preventive detention and of the laws authorizing the exercise of the power of preventive detention in Malaysia. Subsequently, in light of the model preventive detention framework developed in Chap. 3 of this book, an attempt will be made in this chapter to put forward recommendations for introducing meaningful changes in the constitutional provisions governing the exercise of the power of preventive detention in Malaysia. It will be made manifestly evident that a preventive detention framework entrenched in the Federal Constitution providing for effective constraints on the power of preventive detention would not only prevent the possibility of its abuse but also safeguard the enjoyment of the liberty of individuals.

© Springer Nature Singapore Pte Ltd. 2020   113
M. E. Bari, S. Naz, *The Use of Preventive Detention Laws in Malaysia: A Case for Reform*, https://doi.org/10.1007/978-981-15-5811-5_5

5.2   The Quest for a Standard Framework Concerning Preventive Detention

An emergency situation, such as war, external aggression or armed rebellion, poses grave threats to the security and integrity of a nation and, as such, necessitates the resort to effective measures for containing such threats. Since the power of preventive detention enables the executive branch of the government to promptly detain those who are suspected of posing dangers to security of the nation without the constraints of the procedural formalities associated with the ordinary criminal law, its exercise is considered an imperative necessity during emergency situations. However, the broad scope of the power, which permits dispensation of the liberty of individuals without any finding of guilt, often persuades the executive to use the power for imposing unwarranted restrictions on the liberty of individuals in an effort to strengthen its grip on power (See Sects. 2.4, 4.3.1.1 and 4.3.2.4). Accordingly, it is necessary to stipulate effective constitutional safeguards concerning the power of preventive detention for ensuring that response to grave threats facing the life of a nation maintains respect for the human rights of individuals.

However, it should be stressed here that notwithstanding the impact of the extraordinary power of preventive detention on the liberty of individuals and the possibility of abuse of the power, human rights norms developed in the 1950s and 1960s, such as the European Convention on Human Rights, 1950, the International Covenant on Civil and Political Rights, 1966 and the American Convention on Human Rights, 1969, does not stipulate adequate safeguards for mitigating the harshness of the power. For instance, international human rights law does not:

(a) limit the exercise of the extraordinary power of preventive detention to formally declared periods of emergency for obviating the possibility of its use during peacetime for imposing undue restrictions on the liberty of individuals (see Sect. 3.2.1);

(b) stipulate a time limit for informing the detainee of the grounds of his detention in order to facilitate effective representation against the order of detention (see Sect. 3.2.1);

(c) impose a ban on detention incommunicado, which gives rise to the objectionable possibility of torture of detainees, by expressly stipulating that a detainee should be given access to a lawyer and his family members (see Sect. 3.2.1); and

(d) prescribe a maximum period of preventive detention for preventing the possibility of indefinite or prolonged detention of individuals as such detention can lead to the violation of fundamental human rights, such as torture, mistreatment and death of detainees (see Sect. 3.2.1).

Rather the international human rights treaties merely stipulate that the exercise of the power of preventive detention should not be arbitrary. Consequently, taking advantage of such lacunae in the treaties, the state parties to these treaties do not stipulate adequate safeguards in their constitutions for constraining the scope of the power of preventive detention. The absence of effective guarantees in turn leaves the door wide open for executives to use the power of preventive detention as an effective tool for detaining their political adversaries (See Sects. 2.3 and 2.4).

However, the Constitution of some of the modern democracies, such as Pakistan and South Africa, stipulate some of the most fundamental guarantees for not only preventing the abuse of preventive detention but also for ensuring the humane treatment of detainees. For instance, the Constitution of Pakistan, 1973, among other things, obligates the Advisory Board— a quasi-judicial body— to decide the place of detaining an individual in preventive custody and to fix a reasonable maintenance allowance for the members of the family of the detainee (See Sect. 3.3.1(c)). Furthermore, the Pakistani Constitution prescribes a maximum period for keeping an individual in preventive custody (Sect. 3.3.1(d)). Both these safeguards have the merit of guarding against the possibility of the infringement of core rights, such as the right not to be subjected to torture and cruel, inhuman or degrading treatment or punishment and the right to life. On the other hand, the South African Constitution of 1996, goes further than any other modern Constitution for reducing the impact of the exercise of the power of preventive detention on the human rights of individuals. For it not only stipulates extensive safeguards, such as prohibition on detention incommunicado and the right to judicial review within 10 days, but also makes some of the safeguards, such as the right to be informed of the grounds of detention in sufficient detail and the right to be represented by a lawyer, non-derogable during emergency situations in order to obviate the possibility of abuse of the power of preventive detention (See Sect. 3.3.2.1).

Accordingly, this book stresses that a constitutionally entrenched framework concerning preventive detention providing for effective guarantees obviates the possibility of the use of preventive detention for extraneous purposes to impose long-lasting limitations on people's liberty. Such a framework concerning preventive detention should contain the following non-derogable guarantees:

(a) confinement of the use of the power of preventive detention to states of emergency threatening the security and integrity of the nation (See Sect. 3.3(a));
(b) communication of grounds of detention in sufficient detail to a detainee within a specified timeframe in order to facilitate the detainee's right to make an effective representation against detention (See Sect. 3.3(b));
(c) formation of an Advisory Board, which will be independent of the executive, to consider the representation of a detainee within a specific timeframe and to subsequently put forward binding recommendations for the release of a detainee if there are no reasonable grounds for continuing his detention (See Sect. 3.3(c));
(d) prohibition of detention incommunicado in order to obviate the possibility of torture of detainees (See Sect. 3.3(d));
(e) facilitation of a detainee's right to challenge his detention order in pursuance of a writ of *habeas corpus* within the shortest possible timeframe (See Sect. 3.3(e));
(f) prescription of a maximum time-limit for keeping an individual in preventive custody in order to obviate the possibility of indefinite or prolonged detention,

which can lead to the violation of fundamental human rights, such as the right
to freedom from torture (See Sect. 3.3(f)); and

(g) stipulation of a right to claim monetary compensation for arbitrary deprivation
of liberty (See Sect. 3.3(g)).

5.3   The Adequacy of Malaysia's Constitutional Preventive Detention Framework

5.3.1   The Power of Preventive Detention Under the Malaysian Constitution

When the Reid Commission embarked on the journey, as pointed out earlier in Sect.
2.6, of drafting a Constitution for Malaysia, the nation was under a state of emergency which had been declared by the Colonial Government in 1948 to deal with
the threats posed by the communists. In light of the gravity of the threats, which had
not subsided even after Malaysia's emergence as an independent nation, the Reid
Commission recommended the insertion of a provision concerning preventive
detention in the Federal Constitution of Malaysia. However, unlike the colonial
practice in Malaya, as discussed earlier in Sect. 2.5, of confining the exercise of the
power of preventive detention to proclamation of emergency, Article 149(1) of the
Federal Constitution of Malaysia does not confine the exercise of the power of preventive detention to formally declared states of emergency but rather provides the
executive with wide discretion through the use of vague and imprecise words to
determine whether any act is prejudicial to the national security and thereby warrants the exercise of the power of preventive detention. It should be further stressed
here that the Constitution does not afford essential safeguards to individuals kept in
preventive custody for mitigating the harshness of the power of preventive detention. First, the Constitution does not impose an obligation on the detaining authority
to furnish the grounds of detention with sufficient details to the detainee within a
specified timeframe. Second, the Constitution is silent about the timeframe within
which a detainee should be permitted to make a representation before an Advisory
Board, which is constituted by the executive. Third, the Constitution does not confine the composition of the Board solely to individuals who are or have been judges
of the superior courts. Rather it authorizes the executive to choose the composition
of the Board. Thus, the Constitution gives the executive significant leeway to influence the functioning of the Board. Fourth, since the proviso to Article 149(1) of the
Constitution permits preventive detention laws to be inconsistent, among other
things, with the safeguards guaranteed by Article 5, detainees are deprived of essential safeguards, such as the right to challenge the legality of a detention order in
pursuance of a writ of habeas corpus and the right to consult and be defended by a
legal practitioner. Fifth, the Constitution does not outlaw detention incommunicado.
Sixth, the Constitution does not prohibit the detaining authority from keeping an

individual in preventive custody for an indefinite period. Finally, the Constitution does not contain a provision for guaranteeing a detainee's entitlement to monetary compensation in case of unlawful preventive detention (See Sects. 2.6.3 and 4.2).

It is, therefore, evident that the Malaysian Constitution's provisions concerning preventive detention grants wide discretion to the executive to arbitrarily deprive the liberty of individuals. Subsequently, taking advantage of the weaknesses of the constitutional provisions concerning preventive detention, the Parliament has enacted a number of laws concerning preventive detention, namely, the Internal Security Act, 1960 (ISA), the Security Offences (Special Measures) Act, 2012 (SOSMA), the Prevention of Crime Act, 1959 (PCA), as amended in 2014 and 2015, and Prevention of Terrorism Act, 2015 (POTA), enabling succeeding generations of executives to exercise wide powers concerning preventive detention during peacetime for keeping the critics of the party in power behind bars (See Sects. 2.6.3, 4.3.1.1.5, and 4.3.2.4).

5.3.2 Key Characteristics of the Preventive Detention Laws in Malaysia

During 52 years of operation, the ISA, as discussed earlier in Sect. 4.3.1.1, was used as a tool for suppressing the critics of the government of the day. Although the ISA was ultimately repealed in 2012, its wide provisions concerning preventive detention have subsequently been brought back by a series of laws. However, some of these laws concerning preventive detention are far more draconian in nature than the ISA. An attempt will now be made to summarize the key characteristics of the preventive detention laws that have so far been enacted in Malaysia.

5.3.2.1 Vague and Wide Grounds of Detention

The ISA in sections 8 and 73(1) employed vague and broad words, such as "acts prejudicial to the security, maintenance of essential services or economic life", as grounds for authorizing the executive branch of the government to exercise the power of preventive detention. The PCA and POTA, in the same manner as the ISA, also use wide grounds as permitting the exercise of the power of preventive detention. For instance, section 19A(1) of the PCA uses words, such as "in the interest of public order, public security or prevention of crime", for authorizing the Prevention of Crime Board to exercise its discretion to detain individuals. While the POTA in section 13(1) also uses words, such as engagement "in the commission or support of terrorist acts" and "in the interest of the security of Malaysia", for empowering the Prevention of Terrorism Board to deprive individuals of their liberty. Furthermore, the POTA in section 2, as discussed earlier in Sect. 4.3.4.1, does not make any attempt to define the words "terrorism", "terrorist" and "terrorist acts". The use of ambiguous grounds in these statutes in turn gives rise to the fear that the wide powers concerning preventive detention will be used in the same manner as it had been done under the ISA for victimizing political adversaries of the government of the day. In this context, the apprehension expressed by the Malaysian Bar is noteworthy:

> the reach of the legislation is extremely wide and lends itself to abuse. It opens up the possibility that almost anyone could be targeted under POTA. We have seen how ISA, which had been meant to deal with the communist insurgency, was used to stifle political dissent and imprison political opponents.[1]

Additionally, the SOSMA and PCA have authorized the exercise of the power of preventive detention to detain individuals suspected of committing a wide-range of offences, such as smuggling of migrants, human trafficking, and drug trafficking, which are already criminalized under the ordinary criminal law framework and, as such, are not recognized by Article 149(1) of the Constitution as grounds for invoking the power of preventive detention (See Sects. 4.3.2, 4.3.3 and 4.3.4.1).

5.3.2.2 The Body Authorised to Exercise the Power of Preventive Detention

Section 8(1) of the ISA empowered the Home Minister to exercise the power of preventive detention while section 73(1) authorized a police officer to exercise such power. Like section 73(1) of the ISA, the SOSMA under section 4 also grants a police officer the discretion to preventively detain individuals. However, in contrast to the ISA and SOSMA, the PCA and POTA empower the Prevention of Crime Board and the Prevention of Terrorism Board respectively to issue orders for detaining individuals in the interests of public order and public security. The granting of such wide discretion to Boards to dispense with the liberty of individuals is problematic. For the executive is given the unfettered power to appoint the members of the Boards, thereby enabling the former to pack these bodies with loyalists. The executive is further empowered to remove the members of the board at its pleasure. Thus, these Boards remain subservient to the wishes of the executive. Consequently, it can be argued that although the PCA and POTA do not directly authorize the executive to exercise the power of preventive detention, it nevertheless exercises such power indirectly through the Boards (See Sects. 4.3.3 and 4.3.4). This in turn gives rise to the objectionable possibility that Malaysians will be subjected to the same kind of arbitrary exercise of the power of preventive detention, as had been experienced under the ISA. Furthermore, given the Malaysian judiciary's historical reluctance, as pointed out above in Sect. 4.3.1.14, to scrutinize prevention detention orders, it is unlikely that it will thwart the executive's arbitrary encroachment on the liberty of individuals under the PCA and POTA.

---

[1] Thiru (2015).

5.3.2.3   Preventive Detention for an Indefinite or a Prolonged Period

The ISA, as discussed earlier in Sect. 4.3.1.1, in section 8(7) permitted the executive to keep an individual in preventive custody for an indefinite period of time. On the other hand, both the PCA and the POTA, as discussed earlier in Sects. 4.3.3 and 4.3.4, first stipulate that an arrested person can be remanded initially for 21 days and subsequently for a further 38 days on the orders of the Magistrate pending an inquiry into the necessity of continuing the detention. Thus, these statutes authorize the detention of an individual for a period of 59 days on the orders of a Magistrate. Second, both the Acts refrain from stipulating a timeframe within which a person detained on the order of a Magistrate should be brought before an inquiry officer. Third, they do not stipulate a timeframe within which the inquiry officers should submit their reports for the consideration of the Boards. Hence an individual can be kept in custody for a lengthy period even before the Boards are afforded the opportunity to determine whether there is a case for preventively detaining him.

Fourth, upon considering reports for determining whether an individual should be kept in preventive custody, the Prevention of Crime Board and the Prevention of Terrorism Board, as discussed earlier Sects. 4.3.3 and 4.3.4, under the PCA and POTA respectively are empowered to issue detention orders for a period not exceeding 2 years. Such detention orders can be further extended for a period "not exceeding two years" at a time. Thus, like the ISA, both the PCA and the POTA authorize the detention of individuals for an indefinite period of time.

However, it is evident from a perusal of the abovementioned provisions of the PCA and the POTA that they are far more draconian than their predecessor, i.e. the ISA, as they permit detention for a prolonged period even before formal preventive detention orders are issued by the respective Prevention Boards. The unfettered power to deprive individuals of their liberty for a prolonged or an indefinite period of time under the PCA and the POTA in turn grants detaining authorities the opportunity to subject detainees to various methods of torture. For instance, a Report published by the United States Senate in December 2014, as discussed earlier in Sect. 3.2.1, revealed that individuals detained in Guantanamo Bay for prolonged periods were often subjected to various methods of torture, such as waterboarding, sleep deprivation for up to "180 hours" at a time, "rectal hydration or rectal feeding" and "ice water baths".[2]

5.3.2.4   Access to Judicial Review

It may be recalled here from the discussion in Sect. 4.3.1.1.4, that the ISA in section 8B(1) ousted the jurisdiction of the courts to examine the lawfulness of detention orders on substantive grounds. In the same manner as the ISA, section 15A(1) of the

---

[2] Bari (2017), pp. 158.

PCA and section 19(1) of the POTA also exclude the court's jurisdiction to scrutinize detention orders.

5.4 Recommendations: A Constitutionally Entrenched Preventive Detention Framework for Malaysia Providing for Effective Safeguards

The dangers of empowering the executive to exercise the power of preventive detention in an unconstrained manner was aptly summarized by Winston Churchill in the
following manner:

> The power of the executive to cast a man into prison without formulating any charge known
> to the law and particularly to deny him the judgment of his peers is in the highest degree
> odious and the foundation of all totalitarian governments.[3]

It is manifestly evident from the discussion in the preceding Chapters of this
book and summarized above reveals that in the absence of adequate and effective
constitutional safeguards, the Malaysian Parliament has passed one repressive preventive detention law after another permitting the imposition of unwarranted restrictions on the liberty of individuals. Consequently, taking advantage of the weaknesses
of the constitutional provisions concerning preventive detention, succeeding generations of executives in Malaysia have exercised the power of preventive detention
arbitrarily to detain their political adversaries, thereby demonstrating their contempt
towards democratic values, such as respect for the rule of law and the fundamental
human rights of individuals (See Sects. 4.3.1.1 and 4.3.2.4). The broad scope of the
power of preventive detention and its consequent abuse in Malaysia necessitate the
incorporation of the following non-derogable guarantees within the Federal
Constitution of Malaysia, 1957, by means of an amendment:

(a) Confining the Exercise of the Power of Preventive Detention to Formally Declared Periods of Emergency

Taking into account the adverse impact of the exercise of the power of preventive
detention during peacetime under various preventive detention laws, namely the
ISA, SOSMA, PCA and POTA, on the human rights of individuals in Malaysia, it is
imperative that the exercise of the power is confined to formally declared emergencies. For doing so would ensure that the discretion to exercise the extraordinary
power of preventive detention would come to an end as soon as the grave threats
facing the life of a nation is over, thereby ensuring that the power would not be used
in peacetime for indiscriminately depriving individuals of their liberty.

However, merely confining preventive detention to emergencies will not be sufficient for preventing the unrestrained exercise of the power in Malaysia. Rather

---

[3] Quoted in Susskind (2005), pp. 33.

detailed norms should also be inserted in Article 150 of the Constitution providing for legal limits on the executive's unfettered power in Malaysia to proclaim a state of emergency and to, subsequently, continue such an emergency for an indefinite period of time. For unlike the Constitutions of modern democracies, the Malaysian Constitution, as amended in 1963, does not stipulate any grounds for invoking an emergency, thereby authorizing the executive to proclaim an emergency for extraneous purposes without the precondition of grave crises threatening the security of the nation (See Sect. 2.7). Furthermore, the Constitution does not prescribe any mechanism for ensuring the effective scrutiny and timely conclusion of a proclamation of emergency (See Sect. 2.7). Therefore, the proposed amendment to the Constitution should circumscribe the power to proclaim a state of emergency to well-defined circumstances, such as war, external aggression and armed rebellion, which truly endanger the life of the nation, as has been done in India by the Constitution of India, 1950. A proclamation of emergency under the Constitution should also be subjected to periodic review by the increasing supermajorities of the Parliament, as has been done in South Africa (See Sect. 3.3.2.1. Finally, the Constitution should prescribe a maximum time limit of 6 months on the continuance of a proclamation of emergency (See Sect. 2.7). The enumeration of such a time limit would obviate the possibility of an emergency being stretched beyond its imperative necessities.

(b) **Stipulation of a Right to be Informed of the Grounds of Detention within the Shortest Possible Timeframe**

The vague phrase "as soon as may be" used in Article 151(1)(a) of the Constitution of Malaysia as the time period for communicating the grounds of detention to a detainee should be replaced with a specific time-frame of 7 days in order to facilitate an effective representation against the detention order. In order to further facilitate the effectiveness of such representation, the grounds communicated to the detainee should also be sufficiently detailed and should be couched in clear terms. It should also be stressed here that clause 3 of Article 151 of the Constitution, which gives wide discretion to the detaining authority to withhold the grounds of detention if such disclosure is considered to be against the national interest, should also be omitted. For the existence of such a provision renders the right to make a representation before the Board meaningless.

(c) **Stipulation of a Guarantee Permitting the Detainee to Make a Representation before an Advisory Board within a Specified Timeframe**

Notwithstanding the utility of permitting a detainee to make representation against his detention before an Advisory Body, as discussed earlier in Sect. 3.3, within the shortest possible time provides an opportunity for him to satisfy the Board that his detention is not warranted for containing the grave threats posed to the life of the nation, Article 151(1)(b) of the Malaysian Constitution permits the detention of an individual for 3 months without the concurrence of the Board. Thus, the timeframe within which a detainee should be afforded the opportunity to make a representation before the Board should be reduced from 3 months to 10 days, as has been done in the case of the South African Constitution (Sect. 3.3.2.1).

Furthermore, in the same manner as the Constitution of Pakistan, 1973 which authorises the head of the judiciary to constitute the Advisory Board and also confines the membership of such a Board solely to individuals who are or have been judges of the superior courts for preventing the executive from adversely influencing the functioning of the former, Article 151(1)(b) of the Malaysian Constitution should also confine the membership of the Advisory Board solely to those who are or have previously been judges of the superior courts. Furthermore, the Chief Justice of Malaysia— the head of the judiciary— should be entrusted with the responsibility of constituting the Advisory Board (Sects. 3.3.1 and 4.2).

(d) **Stipulation of the Right to Challenge the Legality of the Order of Detention in pursuance of a Writ of Habeas Corpus**

Article 5(2) of the Malaysian Constitution, as discussed earlier in Sect. 2.6.3, authorises the High Court to examine the lawfulness of an individual's detention order in pursuance of a writ of *habeas corpus*. However, the proviso to Article 149(1) of the Constitution permits preventive detention laws to be inconsistent with the guarantees contained in Article 5(2). Consequently, preventive detentions laws enacted by the Parliament, such as the ISA, PCA and POTA, have expressly ousted the jurisdiction of the courts to examine the legality of detention orders on substantive grounds. Therefore, in the first place, the proviso to Article 149(1) should be omitted so as to limit the power of the Parliament to oust the jurisdiction of the courts to examine the legality of detention orders. Furthermore, Article 5(2) of the Constitution should be amended to give a detainee the right to challenge the lawfulness of his detention in pursuance of a writ of *habeas corpus* within 10–30 days of his detention (See Sect. 3.3(c)).

(e) **Stipulation of the Right to Protection from Detention Incommunicado**

By virtue of the proviso to Article 149(1) of the Constitution of Malaysia, the guarantee of the right to consult and to be defended by a lawyer of one's choice contained in Article 5(3) are also not available to an individual kept in preventive custody. Furthermore, the Constitution does not contain any provision guaranteeing a detainee's right to communicate with the members of his family (See Sect. 2.6.3(c) and 4.2(e)). The absence of such guarantees in the Constitution in turn risks facilitating the perpetration of torture of detainees (Sect. 3.2.1). Thus, a provision barring detention incommunicado should be inserted in Article 151 of the Constitution.

(f) **Stipulation of a Maximum Time Limit for Keeping a Detainee in Preventive Custody**

Although indefinite detention facilitates the violation of the fundamental human rights of individuals, such as the right to life and the right not to be subjected to torture, and as such "is anathema in any country which observes the rule of law",[4] the Malaysian Constitution does not stipulate a maximum time period for keeping

---

[4]*A and others v. Secretary of State for the Home Department*, [2004] UKHL 56, paragraph 74.

an individual in preventive custody (Sects. 2.6.3(d) and 4.2(f)). Thus, an overall time limit of 6 months should be inserted in Articles 5 and 149 of the Constitution in order to ensure that the extraordinary power of preventive detention is not arbitrarily used by the party in power to keep the critics of its policies behind bars indefinitely.

(g) Stipulation of a Provision for providing Monetary Compensation

Finally, Article 151 of the Malaysian Constitution should be amended to incorporate a provision providing for monetary compensation to an individual who has been arbitrarily deprived of the right to liberty. The enumeration of such a provision would go a long way to act as an effective check on the executive from exploiting the extraordinary power of preventive detention to impose unwarranted restrictions on the liberty of individuals (See Sect. 3.3(g)).

The incorporation of the above safeguards in the Constitution would prevent security legislation, such as the PCA and POTA, from requiring the complete surrender of the liberty of individuals under the pretense of preserving national security. They also have the merit of precluding the possibility of gross violation of core human rights, such as the right to freedom from torture and mistreatment, and thereby ensure the observance of the rule of law. As Justice Michael Kirby observed:

> There is no doubt that nurturing good governance is essential to ensuring respect for human rights. Without the rule of law, independent courts and the other institutions of a modern society— essential components of good governance— the promise of human rights may remain just that: a promise unfulfilled. Enforcement of fundamental freedoms when it matters may be impossible. The lesson of history is that transparent, responsible, accountable and participatory governance is a prerequisite to enduring respect for human dignity and the defence of human rights.[5]

References

Bari, M. E. (2017). *States of emergency and the law: The experience of Bangladesh.* New York: Routledge.

Kirby, M. (2004) *Human rights— Essential for good governance.* Paper presented at the seminar on good governance practices for the promotion of human rights, Seoul, Korea, 15 September 2004.

Susskind, R. (2005). *The Susskind interviews: Legal experts in changing times.* London: Sweet & Maxwell.

Thiru, S. (2015). *Press release: Prevention of terrorism bill 2015 violates Malaysia's domestic and international commitments, is an affront to the rule of law and is abhorrent to natural justice, The Malaysian Bar.* Available at https://www.malaymail.com/news/what-you-think/2015/04/05/preventive-detention-violates-malaysias-rights-commitments-steven-thiru/872917

---

[5] Kirby (2004), p. 1.

Table of Cases

Decisions of Multilateral Organisations

David Alberto Campora Schweixzer v. Uruguay, Communication No. 66/1980, U.N. Doc. CCPR/C/OP/2 at 90 (1990). (Decisions of Human Rights Committee under the Optional Protocol of ICCPR).

Hugo van Alphen v. The Netherlands, Communication No. 305/1988, U.N. Doc. CCPR/C/39/D/305/1988 (1990) (Decisions of Human Rights Committee under the Optional Protocol of ICCPR).

Domestic Court Judgements

A and others v. Secretary of State for the Home Department, [2004] UKHL 56, paragraph 74. (United Kingdom).

Abdul Ghani Haroon v. Ketua Polis Negara [2001] 2 MLJ 689 (Malaysia).

Abdul Latif Mirza v. Government of Bangladesh, (1979) 31 DLR (AD) 1, 10 (Bangladesh).

AK Gopalan v. State of Madras [1950] SCR 88 (India).

Aruna Sen v. Government of Bangladesh [1974] 3 CLC (HCD) 1 (Bangladesh).

Borhan Hj Daud & Ors v. Abd Malek Hussin [2010] 8 CLJ 656 (Malaysia).

Dalip Bhagwan Singh v. Public Prosecutor [1997] 4 CLJ 645 (Malaysia).

Ferreira v. Levin NO and Others; *Vryenhoek v Powell NO and Others*, 1996(1) SA 984 (CC), 1996(1) BCLR 1 (CC) at 1015 (para 51) (South Africa).

Gurcharan Singh Bachittar Singh v. Penguasa, Tempat Tahanan Perlindungan Kamunting, Taiping & Ors [2002] 4 MLJU 255 (Malaysia).

Her Majesty's Treasury v. Ahmad, etc, [2010] UKSC 2, para 6 (United Kingdom).

In Re: Berubari Union Case, AIR 1960 SC 845 (India).

© Springer Nature Singapore Pte Ltd. 2020

M. E. Bari, S. Naz, *The Use of Preventive Detention Laws in Malaysia: A Case for Reform*, https://doi.org/10.1007/978-981-15-5811-5

Kandupillai Krishnan v. Timbalan Menteri Dalam Negeri, Malaysia & Ors [2004] 1 MLJ 85 (Malaysia).

Karam Singh v. Menteri Hal Ehwal Dalam Negeri (Minister of Home Affairs) [1969] 2 MLJ 129 (Malaysia).

Kerajaan Malaysia & Ors. v. Nasharuddin Nasir [2004] 1 CLJ 81 (Malaysia).

Khan Ghulam Mohammed Khan Loondkhawar v. The State [1957] PLD Lah. 497 (Pakistan).

Liversidge v. Anderson [1942] AC 206 (United Kingdom).

Mir Abdul Baqi Baluch v. Government of Pakistan [1968] PLD (SC) 313 (Pakistan).

Mohamad Ezam Mohd Noor v. Ketua Polis Negara [2002] 4 CLJ 309 (Malaysia).

Mohamad Ezam Mohd Nor v. Ketua Polis Negara [2002] 4 CLJ 309 (Malaysia).

Mohd Ezam Mohd Noor v. Ketua Polis Negara & Other Appeals [2002] 4 CLJ 309, 360 (Malaysia).

Nasharuddin Nasir v. Kerajaan Malaysia & Ors (No. 2) [2003] 1 CLJ 353 (Malaysia).

Ng Boon Hock v. Penguasa, Tempat Tahanan Perlindungan Kamunting, Taiping & Ors [1998] MLJ 174 (Malaysia).

Raja Petra Raja Kamarudin v. Menteri Hal Ehwal Dalam Negeri [2008] 1 LNS 920 (Malaysia).

Re Tan Sri Raja Khalid bin Raja Raja Harun; Inspector-General of Police v. Tan Sri Raja Khalid bin (1988) 1 MLJ 182 (Malaysia).

Rex v. Halliday [1917] AC 260 (United Kingdom).

Rowshen Bijaya Shaukat Ali Khan v. Government of East Pakistan, [1965] 17 PLD 241, 247 and 256 (Pakistan).

Sachs v. Minister of Justice (1934) AD 11 (A) (South Africa).

Sampath Kumar v. Union of India [1987] SC 386 (India).

State of Bombay v. Atma Ram Shridhar Vaidya A.I.R. 1951 S.C. 157 (India).

Tan Sri Norian Mai & Ors v. Chua Tian Chang & Ors [2015] 4 MLJ 464, 485 (Malaysia).

Tan Sri Raja Khalid Raja Harun v. the Inspector-General of Police [1987] CLJ (Rep) 1014 (Malaysia).

Teh Cheng Poh v. Public Prosecutor [1979] 1 MLJ 50 (Malaysia).

Teh Cheng Poh v. Public Prosecutor [1979] 1 MLJ 50, 54 (Malaysia).

Theresa Lim Chin Chin v. Inspector General of Police [1988] 1 LNS 132 (Malaysia).

Theresa Lim Chin Chin v. Inspector General of Police [1988] 1 MLJ 293 (Malaysia).

Bibliography

Articles/Books/Reports/Research Papers

Ackerman, B. (2006). *Before the next attack: Preserving civil liberties in an age of terrorism* (p. 54). Yale University Press.

Administrative arrangement between the Government of Malaysia and the Communist Party of Malaya Pursuant to the agreement to terminate hostilities. Available at http://theirwords.org/media/transfer/doc/my_cpm_1989_01-2aa2b0cc70df62b0ef0b5f519d5b3065.pdf

Aldred, G., & Wynn, J. (2012). *It might have happened to your: Britain's "Guantanamo Bay" imprisonment without trial in WW2.*

Ashutosh, D. (2014). *Law of preventive detention* (p. 24). Universal Law Publishing Co.

Bari, M. E. (2011). *Substantive independence of the judiciary under the constitutions of Malaysia and Bangladesh: A comparative study* (pp. 53–54). LLM Dissertation. University of Malaya, Kuala Lumpur, Malaysia.

Bari, M. E. (2017a). Preventive detention laws in Bangladesh and their increased use during emergencies: A proposal for reform. *Oxford University Commonwealth Law Journal, 17*(1), 45–46.

Bari, M. E. (2017b). *States of emergency and the law: The experience of Bangladesh* (pp. 39, 64, 95, 27, 430). Routledge.

Basu, D. D., & Nandi, A. K. (2000). *Administrative law* (p. 544). Kolkata: Kamal Law House.

Bonner, D. (1985). *Emergency powers in peacetime* (p. 2). Sweet & Maxwell.

Commission on Human Rights. (1999). *Report of the working group on arbitrary detention addendum report on the mission to Peru, E/CN.4/199963/Add.2.* Available at https://daccess-ods.un.org/TMP/3248046.3385582.html

Constituent Assembly Debates. 1949. *India* (Vol. IX, pp. 1505–1508) (Lok Sabha Secretariat).

Cook, H. (1992). Preventive detention – International standards and the protection of the individual. In S. Frankowski & D. Shelton (Eds.), *Preventive detention: A comparative and international law perspectives* (pp. 11, 25). Springer.

de Zayas, A. (2005). Human Rights and Indefinite Detention. *International Review of the Red Cross, 87*(15), 19.

Despouy, L. (UN. Special Rapporteur on Human Rights and Emergency). (1998). *Annual report of the special rapporteur of the sub-commission on prevention of discrimination and protection*

of minorities on human rights and states of emergency 26, 66. UN Doc E/CN.4/Sub.2/1989/
SR.32. Available at https://digitallibrary.un.org/record/253914?ln=en

Drummond, S., & Hawkins, D. (1970). The Malaysian elections of 1969: An analysis of the campaign and the results. *Asian Survey 10*(4), 320, 322.

Dyzenhaus, D. (2010). *Hard cases in wicked legal systems: Pathologies of legality* (Part XI). Oxford University Press.

Federation of Malaya Constitutional Commission (Reid Commission). (1957). *Report of the federation of Malaya constitutional commission.*

FIDH. (2016). *Worldwide movement for human rights, Malaysia: Continued arbitrary detention and solitary confinement of Maria Chin Abdullah, Chairperson of Bersih 2.0.* Available at https://www.fidh.org/en/issues/human-rights-defenders/malaysia-continued-arbitrary-detention-and-solitary-confinement-of

Fitzpatrick, J. (1994). *Human rights in crisis: The international system for protecting rights during states of emergency* (pp. 45–46). Philadelphia: University of Pennsylvania Press.

Harding, A. J., & Hatchard, J. (1993). Introduction. In A. J. Harding & J. Hatchard (Eds.), *Preventive detention and security law: A comparative survey* (p. 5, 6, 8). Martinus Nijhoff Publishers.

Hartman, J. F. (1981). Derogation from human rights treaties in public emergencies. *Harvard International Law Journal, 22*(1), 17.

Hartman, J. (1985). Working paper for the committee of experts on the Article 4 derogation provision. *Human Rights Quarterly, 7*, 115–118.

Heap, M., & Morgans, H. (2007). Language policy and SASL: Interpreters in the public service. In B. Watermeyer et al. (Eds.), *Disability and social change: A South African agenda* (p. 134). HSRC Press.

Hickling, H. R. (1962). The first five years of the federation of Malaya constitution. *Malaya Law Review, 4*, 183.

Human Rights Commission of Malaysia. (2003). *Review of the Internal Security Act, 1960.* Available at http://www.suhakam.org.my/wp-content/uploads/2013/12/review-of-the-ISA-1960.pdf

Human Rights Watch. (2004). *In the Name of Security Counterterrorism and Human Rights Abuses Under Malaysia's Internal Security Act.* Available at https://www.hrw.org/reports/2004/malaysia0504/malaysia0504.pdf

In Sofiah Jewa Tunku. et al. (Eds.), *Tun Mohammed Suffian's: An introduction to the constitutional of Malaysia* (3rd ed., pp. 11–14). Pacifica Publications.

International Commission of Jurists. (1983). *States of emergency: Their impact on human rights* (pp. 394, 429, 430).

International Commission of Jurists. (2012). *Submission to the working group on arbitrary detention: The definition and scope of arbitrary deprivation of liberty in customary international law.* Available at http://icj.wpengine.netdna-cdn.com/wp-content/uploads/2012/06/Submission-working-Group-detention-analysis-brief-2012.pdf

Iyer, V. (1999). States of emergency— Moderating their effects on human rights. *Dalhousie Law Journal, 22*, 134–135.

Iyer, V. (2000). *States of emergency: The Indian experience* (p. 109). Butterworths India.

James, T., & Jeffery, B. (2013). Preventive detention in Malaysia: Constitutional and judicial obstacles to reform and suggestions for the future. *Georgia Journal of International & Comparative Law, 41*(535), 549–550.

Jayakumar, S. (1978). Emergency powers in Malaysia: Development of the law 1957–1977. *MAL. Law Journal, 1*, 9–24.

Kirby, M. (2004). *Human rights— Essential for good governance.* Paper presented at the seminar on good governance practices for the promotion of human rights, Seoul, Korea.

Kirk, J. (1997). Constitutional guarantees, characterization, and the concept of proportionality. *Melbourne University Law Review, 21*, 2.

Lee, H. P. (1999). Constitutional heads and judicial intervention. In W. M. Aun (Ed.), *Law in contemporary Malaysia* (p. 5). Selangor: Addison Wesley Longman.

Londras, F. De. (2011). *Detention in the 'War on Terror': Can Human Rights Fight Back?* (pp. 36, 54). Cambridge University Press.

Martinez, J. S. (2005-06). Inherent executive power: A Comparative Perspective. *Yale Law Journal, 115*, 2480, 2496.

Memorandum by Tunku Abdul Rahman. (1955). *Malayan Chinese Association Files*. MCA Headquarters, Kuala Lumpur, PH/A/0084.

Meron, T. (1986). *Human rights Law Making in the United Nations: A critique of instruments and process* (p. 83). Oxford: Clarendon Press.

Munim F. K. M. A. (1975). *Rights of The Citizens Under the Constitution and Law* (p. 333). Bangladesh Institute of Law and International Affairs.

Office of the United Nations High Commissioner for Human Rights. (2013a). *Statement of the United Nations Special Rapporteur on torture at the Expert Meeting on the situation of detainees held at the U.S. Naval Base at Guantanamo Bay*. Available at http://newsarchive.ohchr.org/en/NewsEvents/Pages/DisplayNews.aspx?NewsID=13859&LangID=E

Office of the United Nations High Commissioner for Human Rights. (2013b). *Statement of the United Nations Special Rapporteur on torture at the Expert Meeting on the situation of detainees held at the U.S. Naval Base at Guantanamo Bay*. Available at http://newsarchive.ohchr.org/en/NewsEvents/Pages/DisplayNews.aspx?NewsID=13859&LangID=E

Oraa, J. (1995). *Human rights in States of Emergency in International Law* (pp. 106, 113). Clarendon Press.

Parliamentary Debates: Dewan Rakyat (House of Representatives).

Rudolph, H. (1984). The judicial review of administrative detention orders in Israel. In Y. Dinstein (Ed.), *Israel Yearbook on Human Rights* (p. 12). Martinus Nijhoff Publishers.

Sheridan, L. A. (1961). *Malaya and Singapore, The Borneo Territories: The development of their laws and constitutions* (p. 562). Steven & Sons.

Suara Rakyat Malaysia (Suaram). (2014). *Malaysia: Human Rights Report Overview* 4. Available at https://www.suaram.net/wp-content/uploads/2018/02/HR2014-lowres.pdf

Suara Rakyat Malaysia (Suaram). (2015). *Malaysia Human Rights Report VII*. Available At http://www.suaram.net/wordpress/wp-content/uploads/2017/02/HR2015.pdf

Susskind, R. (2005). *The Susskind interviews: Legal experts in changing times* (p. 33). Sweet & Maxwell.

UN Office of the High Commissioner for Human Rights (OHCHR). (2005). *Human rights – A handbook for parliamentarians, No. 8 – 2005* (p. 5). Available at http://www.refworld.org/docid/46cea90d2.html

United Nations. Commission on Human Rights. (1949). *Summary record of the 126th meeting held at Lake Success, New York, on Monday, 14 June 1949 [International Covenant on Civil and Political Rights]*, E/CN.4/SR.126. See French and US alternative proposals under the Covenant, UN Doc.E/CN.4/324 (1949) and 325 (1949).

United Nations. (2003). *Human rights and arrest, pre-trial detention and administrative detention – Human rights in the administration of justice: A manual on human rights for Judges, Prosecutors and Lawyers*. Available at http://www.ohchr.org/Documents/Publications/training9chapter5en.pdf

United Nations Human Rights Committee. (2013). *International commission of jurists: Initial comments on draft general comment 35 on Article 9 of the International Covenant on Civil and Political Rights*. Available at http://www.ohchr.org/Documents/HRBodies/CCPR/GConArticle9/ICJ_GCArticle9.pdf

United Nations Human Rights Council. (2010). *Report of the working group on arbitrary detention* (p. 76), A/HRC/13/30. Available at https://www1.umn.edu/humanrts/wgad/2010report.pdf

United Nations Human Rights Council. (2012). *International commission of jurists, submission to the working group on arbitrary detention: The definition and scope of arbitrary deprivation of liberty in Customary International Law*. Available at http://icj.wpengine.netdna-cdn.com/wp-content/uploads/2012/06/Submission-working-Group-detention-analysis-brief-2012.pdf

United Nations Office on Drugs and Crime. (2009). *Handbook on Criminal Justice, Responses to Terrorism* 104. Available at Http://Www.Unodc.Org/Documents/Terrorism/Handbook_On_Criminal_Justice_Responses_To_Terrorism_En.Pdf

United States Senate Select Committee on Intelligence. (2012). *Committee study of the Central Intelligence Agency's Detention and Interrogation Program: Findings and Conclusions* 3–4. Available at https://www.amnestyusa.org/pdfs/sscistudy1.pdf

US Department of State. (2020). *Background note: Malaysia*. Available at http://www.state.gov/r/pa/ei/bgn/2777.htm

Webber, D.. (2016). *Preventive detention of terror suspects: A New Legal Framework* (p. 5). Routledge.

Yatim, R. (1995). *Freedom under executive power in Malaysia: A study of executive supremacy* (pp. 293, 369). Endowment Publications.

List of National Constitutions and Constitutional Amendments

Constitution (Amendment) Act, 1978 (Malaysia) (effective date 15 May 1981).

Constitution (Amendment) Act, 1994 (Malaysia) (effective date 24 June 1994).

Constitution of Poland, 1997 (Poland) (effective date 2 April 1997). Available at https://www.sejm.gov.pl/prawo/konst/angielski/kon1.htm

Constitution (Amendment) Act, 1978 (Malaysia) (effective date 31 December 1978).

Constitution (Amendment) Act, 1960 (Malaysia) (effective date 31 May 1960).

Constitution of Bangladesh, 1972 (Bangladesh) (effective date 16 December 1972). Available at http://bdlaws.minlaw.gov.bd/act-367.html

Constitution of India, 1950 (India) (effective date 26 January 1950). Available at https://www.india.gov.in/my-government/constitution-india/constitution-india-full-text

Constitution of Islamic Republic of Pakistan, 1973 (Pakistan) (effective date 12 April 1973). Available at http://www.na.gov.pk/uploads/documents/1333523681_951.pdf

Constitution of the Republic of South Africa, 1996 (South Africa) (effective date 4 February 1997). Available at https://www.gov.za/documents/constitution-republic-south-africa-1996

Federal Constitution of Malaysia, 1957 (Malaysia) (effective date 31 August 1957). Available at http://www.agc.gov.my/agcportal/uploads/files/Publications/FC/Federal%20Consti%20(BI%20text).pdf

Statutes/Rules/Treaties/Conventions/General Comments/ Principles

American Convention on Human Rights (ACHR), opened for signature on 22 November 1969, 1144 UNTS 123 (entered into force on 18 July 1978).

Defence of the Realm Act, 1914 (United Kingdom) (commencement date 7 August 1914).

Emergency Regulations Ordinance, 1948 (Malaysia).

European Convention for the Protection of Human Rights and Fundamental Freedoms (ECHR), opened for signature 4 November 1950, 213 UNTS 222 (entered into force on 3 September 1953).

General Comment No. 8: Right to Liberty and Security of Persons, U.N. Human Rights Committee, U.N. Doc. HRI/GEN/1/Rev.7 (Adopted on Sixteenth Session, 1982). Available at http://www.derechos.org/nizkor/ley/doc/obgen2en.html

Internal Security Act, 1960 (Malaysia) (effective date 1 August 1960).

International Covenant on Civil and Political Rights (ICCPR), opened for signature on 16 December 1966, 999 UNTS 171 (entered into force on 23 March 1976).

Malaysia Penal Code, 1936 (Malaysia) (effective date throughout Malaysia – 31 March 1976).

National Security Act, 1980 (India) (effective date 27 December 1980).

Prevention of Crime (Amendment and Extension) Act, 2014 (Malaysia) (effective date 2 April 2014).

Security of Pakistan Act, 1952 (Pakistan) (effective date 5 May 1952).

Security Offences (Special Measures) Act, 2012 (SOSMA) (Malaysia). (effective date 31 July 2012).

Siracusa Principles on the Limitation and Derogation Provisions in the International Covenant on Civil and Political Rights, UN Commission on Human Rights, E/CN.4/1985/4 (Publication Date – 28 September 1984). Available at available at: https://www.refworld.org/docid/4672bc122.html

Special Measures Against Terrorism in Foreign Countries Act, 2015 (Malaysia).

Special Powers Act, 1974 (Bangladesh) (effective date 9 February 1974).

The Anti-Money Laundering, Anti- Terrorism Financing and Proceeds of Unlawful Activities Act of 2001 (Malaysia) (effective date 15 January 2002).

The Body of Principles for the Protection of All Persons under Any Form of Detention or Imprisonment, General Assembly resolution 43/173 (Adopted on 9 December 1988).

The Paris Minimum Standards of Human Rights Norms in a State of Emergency, Committee on the Enforcement of Human Rights Law, International Law Association (Approved at the 61st Conference of the International Law Association, 1984).

The Prevention of Crime Act, 1959 (PCA) (Malaysia) (effective date 1 April 1959).

The Prevention of Terrorism Act, 2015 (POTA) (Malaysia) (effective date 1 September 2015).

Websites/Internet Materials

Amnesty International UK. *Press Release: UK Lords Ruling: Three Years Too Late for Internees.* www.amnesty.org.uk/press-releases/uk-lords-ruling-three-years-too-late-internees. Accessed 10 Dec 2013.

Amnesty International. *Urgent action. Free politician held for exposing corruption.* https://www.amnesty.org/download/Documents/ASA2824892015ENGLISH.pdf

Hector, C. *Detention without trial laws in Malaysia.* http://www.malaysianbar.org.my/human_rights/detention_without_trial_laws_in_malaysia_.html

Human Rights Watch website at https://www.hrw.org

Human Rights Watch. Malaysia: Reject security bill extension – Let abusive detention provision lapse. https://www.hrw.org/news/2017/03/30/malaysia-reject-security-bill-extension

Hynes, G. (2017). *Defence of the Realm Act.* Available on https://encyclopedia.1914-1918-online.net/article/defence_of_the_realm_act_dora

International Federation for Human Rights website at https://www.fidh.org/en/

Ki-Moon Ban. *Secretary-General's statement at the Special Meeting of the Counter-Terrorism Committee with Regional Organizations.* http://www.un.org/sg/STATEMENTS/index.asp?nid=275

Kumar, K. *IGP: New security laws "better than ISA".* http://www.themalaymailonline.com/malaysia/article/igp-new-security-laws-better-than-isa

Malaysiakini. *Suhakam: SOSMA could violate human rights.* http://freemalaysiakini2.blogspot.com/2013/07/suhakam-sosma-could-violate-human-rights.html

Pandey, G. *Article 370: What happened with Kashmir and why it matters.* https://www.bbc.com/news/world-asia-india-49234708

Ramakrishnan, P. *Scrap the ISA Advisory Board.* http://aliran.com/archives/ms/2003/0115.html

Saravanamuttu, J. *Operation Lalang revisited: A call for the repeal of ISA.* http://aliran.com/aliran-monthly/2008/2008-8/operation-lalang-revisited-a-call-for-the-repeal-of-isa/

Sekhri, A.. *Not fair, just or reasonable.* https://www.thehindu.com/opinion/op-ed/not-fair-just-or-reasonable/article30905962.ece

Singh, B.. *New law gives Malaysia teeth in fight against terror.* http://www.todayonline.com/world/asia/new-law-gives-malaysia-teeth-fight-against-terror

Singh, S. *AG drops charges against 12 sccused of supporting LTTE.* https://www.nst.com.my/news/crime-courts/2020/02/567658/ag-drops-charges-against-12-accused-supporting-ltte

Soong,K.K.*Detentionwithouttrialbiggestobstacletotransformation.*http://www.freemalaysiatoday.com/category/opinion/2016/11/23/detention-without-trial-biggest-obstacle-to-transformation/

Spiegel, M., *Smoke and mirrors: Malaysia's "New" Internal Security Act.* http://www.hrw.org/sites/default/files/related_material/2012_Malaysia_EastWest.pdf

Staff Reporter. SC seeks J&K admin's response on plea against Mehbooba Mufti's detention under PSA. https://timesofindia.indiatimes.com/india/sc-seeks-jk-admins-response-on-plea-against-mehbooba-muftis-detention-under-psa/articleshow/74317822.cms

Suara Rakyat Malaysia (SUARAM) website at https://www.suaram.net

Sydney Morney Herald. Royal revolutionary pays price for backing Anwar. http://www.smh.com.au/articles/2002/03/29/1017206152563.html

The Guardian. Malaysia arrests 17 for alleged terrorist attack plot in Kuala Lumpur. https://www.theguardian.com/world/2015/apr/06/malaysia-arrests-17-for-alleged-terrorist-attack-plot-in-kuala-lumpur

The Guardian. Thousands call for Malaysian Prime Minister Najib Razak to Quit. https://www.theguardian.com/world/2016/nov/19/thousands-call-for-malaysian-prime-minister-najib-razak-to-quit

The Khilafah. Malaysia's Prevention of Terrorism Act 2015: Another step that pleases America. http://www.khilafah.com/malaysias-prevention-of-terrorism-act-2015-another-step-that-pleases-america/

The Malaysian Insider. Parliament passes controversial anti-terrorism law by 79 to 60 votes. https://sg.news.yahoo.com/parliament-passes-controversial-anti-terrorism-law-79-60225022379.html

The Star Online. PM announces repeal of ISA, three emergency proclamation. http://www.thestar.com.my/story/?file=%2F2011%2F9%2F15%2Fnation%2F20110915205714

The Sun Daily. Appeals court awards RM4.55m to Tian Chua, Hishamuddin Rais, 3 others. http://www.thesundaily.my/news/1265144

The Sun Daily. Court rules charge against Khairuddin, Chang does not fall under SOSMA. http://www.thesundaily.my/news/1614590

The Telegraph. Professor Hugh Hickling. http://www.telegraph.co.uk/news/obituaries/1548788/Professor-Hugh-Hickling.html

Thiru, S. *Press release: Prevention of Terrorism Bill 2015 violates Malaysia's domestic and international commitments, is an Affront to the Rule of Law and is Abhorrent to Natural Justice.* https://www.malaysianbar.org.my/article/news/press-statements/press-statements/press-release-prevention-of-terrorism-bill-2015-violates-malaysia-s-domestic-and-international-commitments-is-an-affront-to-the-rule-of-law-and-is-abhorrent-to-natural-justice

Tisdall, S. *Malaysia uses specious terrorism threat to regress on human rights.* https://www.theguardian.com/world/2015/apr/07/malaysia-najib-razak-terrorism-threat-human-rights-detention-without-trial

United Nations Human Rights, Office of the High Commissioner website at https://www.ohchr.org/EN/pages/home.aspx

United Nations website at https://www.un.org/en/

United Nations Treaty Collection website at https://treaties.un.org/Pages/ViewDetails.aspx?src=TREATY&mtdsg_no=IV-3&chapter=4&clang=_en

United Nations Working Group on Arbitrary Detention website at https://www.ohchr.org/EN/Issues/Detention/Pages/WGADIndex.aspx

US Department of State website at https://www.state.gov

Wright, T., & Clark, S. *Investigators believe money flowed to Malaysian Leader Najib's accounts Amid 1MDB Probe.* https://www.wsj.com/articles/SB10130211234592774869404581083700187014570

Zarifi, S. *Open letter to Parliament on POTA.* http://icj2.wpengine.com/wp-content/uploads/2015/04/Malaysia-Open-Letter-to-Parliament-on-POTA-Advocacy-open-letter-2015-ENG.pdf

Zeldin, W. *Malaysia: Anti-Terrorism Law proposed.* http://www.loc.gov/lawweb/servlet/lloc_news?disp3_l205404242_text

Zolkepli, F. *Matthias Chang Detained under SOSMA.* http://www.thestar.com.my/news/nation/2015/10/08/matthias-chang-detained-under-sosma/

Zurairi, A. R. *Lawyer: Maria Chin to be held for 28 days under SOSMA.* http://www.themalaymailonline.com/malaysia/article/lawyer-maria-chin-to-be-held-full-28-days-under-sosma#l4WzKEhEcH54Bmdd.97

Printed by Printforce, the Netherlands